GETTING
BEHIND THE RESUME
Interviewing Today's Candidates

Jim Kennedy

Kay Sprinkel Grace
Contributing Editor

Prentice Hall Information Services

Acknowledgments

Several individuals influenced this book, and I want to thank them publicly.

Kay Sprinkel Grace's editorial contribution to the entire manuscript supports the book's overall readability and cohesion. Her chapters on intuition and listening skills are representative of Kay's personal strengths.

Karen Brahms provided a number of the strategies offered in the chapter on reference checking. This is one of the most demanding tasks facing today's interviewers, and is usually the weakest link in the hiring process.

Martin Delaney suggested the techniques contained in the chapter on consultative selling, which shows how to convince top candidates to accept your offer.

Dr. John Drake, author (*Interviewing for Managers*, New York: Amacom, 1982) and industrial psychologist, first coached me in effective interviewing techniques some 20 years ago. A number of his ideas have stood the test of time and are incorporated in this book.

Many other professionals have revealed their ideas to me while participating in my seminars over the past dozen years. It would be difficult to acknowledge them all by name. They've described successfully tested techniques from a wide range of organizations, many experiencing recent culture change, and all facing polished, savvy candidates.

Jim Kennedy

Contents

SPECIAL SITUATIONS

Contents

Introduction

Interviewing:
A Critical Management Skill

I learned to figure people out pretty quickly. That's an important skill to have, because the most important thing any manager can do is hire the right new people.*

Lee Iacocca

Managers who are exceptional interviewers have a career-long advantage over those who never learn or develop interviewing skills. Simply put, they tend to produce more because they have better people—those they select and convince to join their teams.

Making the right hiring decisions can help your organization outperform your competition. As an executive search professional once put it: "Class A people hire Class A people. Class B people hire Class B people." In other words, good hiring has a ripple effect throughout the organization. Good hiring requires interviewing, and this management skill has never been more important than it is today.

---

*Lee Iacocca with William Novak, *Iacocca: an Autobiography*. Copyright © 1984 by Lee Iacocca. Published by Bantam Books, Inc.

Major shifts in demographics and the economy have affected the job marketplace and place new demands on the interviewing skills of experienced managers. Bridging these trends—economic and demographic—is the growing recognition that people and jobs must fit together. The culture of an organization influences the type of people who will do well there. Corporate culture is a powerful force that must be factored into good interviewing.

DEMOGRAPHIC AND ECONOMIC TRENDS

"Baby boomers"—those born between 1946 and 1964—are becoming a larger part of the workforce. They are well-educated and have high expectations for their careers. At the same time, global competition has placed economic pressures on productivity. In capital-intensive businesses, the best companies are squeezing the last penny out of production, purchasing, and distribution systems. In the more rapidly growing service sector, human resource costs are typically the major component in the pricing of services delivered. The best available people must be hired and retained so the organization is optimally staffed and not plagued by costly turnover.

The long-term trend for businesses today is to "run lean." Many are downsizing their operations. Most often the work doesn't go away; there are simply fewer people to do it. Companies that have gone through painful downsizing will resist re-staffing to former levels. They expect more from their employees and will continue to seek and promote only the best.

These economic trends restrict career opportunities for these millions of well-educated "boomers" whose swelling of the job marketplace was described by *The Wall Street Journal* as a "pig moving through a python." These men and women are competing more aggressively for better jobs. They are devouring books and training courses that help them prepare flawless resumes and take control of job interviews.

Many of these candidates spend more time preparing an answer to a single question they anticipate they will be asked than managers spend preparing for the entire interview. Some schools, particularly at the graduate level, videotape student interviews and then provide feedback to help fine-tune the skills of their graduates. They are told what questions to anticipate and how to respond to them.

HOW THIS BOOK CAN HELP INTERVIEWERS

To make the right hiring decision, the interviewer must maintain control of the interview. Yet, in today's competitive marketplace, busy managers find selection interviewing a necessary but time-consuming management task for which they are poorly prepared. They find themselves face-to-face with candidates who are polished, skillful interviewers easily able to take the upper hand.

The challenge for these busy managers is to separate strong performers from those who are merely good at interviewing.

Given the marketplace realities, it is not enough to know basic interviewing techniques. Interviewers must also know how to take the obvious qualities suggested by someone's education and experience—what is listed on the resume—and predict how that person will perform a given job within the culture of the organization and the changing demands of the industry.

The major goal of this book is to give managers confidence and techniques to control every interview they conduct and learn what they need to know about today's candidates. This has been done in as simple and practical a format as possible.

When new knowledge needs arise in organizations, managers historically invest time in training to learn new skills. On-the-job time is invested to master new computerized systems, productivity improvement programs, consultative selling techniques and other programs that have a traceable relationship to the bottom line.

A commensurate willingness to invest similar time to learn effective interviewing techniques is rarely encountered in most organizations, despite the fact that hiring someone is really a very expensive purchasing decision.

Because selection interviewing has not been viewed as a core skill, managers seldom receive feedback from within their organizations about their interviewing effectiveness. This leads to complacency on the part of interviewers that can put the candidate in control of the interview. Satisfaction with their own interviewing skills underlies managers' resistance to learning how to conduct a more revealing interview.

Getting Behind the Resume is based on the idea that interviewing candidates requires separating *what* candidates have done from *how* they have done it. Basic behavioral interviewing concepts are presented within the framework of a simple Interviewing Model that enables interviewers to gather examples and form premises about the Resume Factor (*what* candidates have done) and three Performance Factors (*how* they have done it). To this model are added methods for assessing corporate culture and using it as an integral part of candidate/job profiles. From these premises, future on-the-job behavior can more accurately be predicted. The balance of the techniques, skills, and applications of the model in the book are built around these basic concepts.

Hiring the wrong person can cost an organization a year's salary or more. Time, budget, momentum, and professional image can all be damaged as a result. Today's managers are challenged by demographic and economic trends affecting the marketplace, and by well-prepared candidates who know how to take control of the interview. The powerful and pragmatic ideas presented in *Getting Behind the Resume* should help interviewers meet this challenge and hire the right person for the job.

1

Challenges for Experienced Interviewers

Often the employer representative . . . will know very little about good interviewing techniques.*

Tom Jackson
Guerrilla Tactics in the Job Market

T he longest train ride of my life was only two hours long, but it followed a full day of interviewing for which I was completely unprepared.

The division marketing manager, who had just hired me the week before at General Foods, sat down next to me on the 6 p.m. train from Philadelphia to New York.

"Well, Jim," he said, "you've just interviewed thirteen MBAs at Wharton. Tell me about them."

My day, which had started with my first interview at 8:30 a.m., was a complete blur to me. I could hardly distinguish the thirteen candidates from one another. Now I was supposed to talk about each

---

*Tom Jackson, *Guerrilla Tactics in the Job Market* (New York: Bantam Books, 1978).

of them! I was really feeling very exposed, for I had received no training in interviewing techniques before this marathon interviewing experience.

I thought I could rescue the moment by referring to the scribbled notes I'd taken on the margins of each candidate's resume. I jumped right into my description of each student.

"Well, let's see . . . the first guy I interviewed at 8:30 did his undergraduate work at Brown. He majored in political science. Then he worked in sales for two years at IBM. At Wharton he's concentrating on marketing and is president of the Marketing Club. He looks pretty good."

"Why?" asked the division marketing manager.

"Because he's got good marketing credentials," I replied.

"But all you've told me is just what's on his resume," he responded. "What did you learn about him as a person? What kind of marketing judgment does he have? What motivates him? Is he a good strategic thinker? How will he fit into General Foods?"

In truth, I could not answer any of his questions about the student I'd interviewed at 8:30 or any of the twelve others on my schedule. I had just spent nine hours in a tiny cubicle "interviewing" thirteen MBAs, yet I could not describe any of them as people or in any kind of depth. All I had done was gather facts and data, most of which was already listed on their resumes.

Instead of interviewing, I had merely confirmed available information. It would have been less expensive and just as effective for General Foods to have had the student resumes sent to company headquarters in White Plains than to send me to Wharton.

It was a long, awkward, and embarrassing train ride back to New York. What a terrible way to start a new job!

What had gone wrong? *By failing to get behind the resume and really interview those candidates, I had plunged head first into one of the most common mistakes in American business.* I had been given the responsibility for interviewing others but had received no training or coaching in this critical management skill. I did not know what to look for in an interview, nor how to obtain it with effective questions and probes.

When I was given the interviewing assignment a few days earlier, no one bothered to ask if I knew how to interview or whether I had any actual experience at it. (It was therefore easy for me to assume my new employer was wise in his assumption that someone as bright and eager as I could certainly handle such a simple task as selection interviewing!)

NO FORMAL TRAINING IN INTERVIEWING

Despite the fact that hiring the right new people is one of the most important tasks a manager faces, the vast majority have never had formal training in effective interviewing techniques. Most people learn how to interview in a "sink or swim" manner. It starts when their supervisor says, "From now on you will be doing some interviewing for us. Here's the resume of a guy coming in tomorrow—why don't you talk to him and see what you think."

This, then, is the first challenge experienced managers face. They begin a lifetime of interviewing others with no real training. Because they have not learned the strategies of interviewing, they tend to underestimate the number and importance of the skills required to conduct an effective interview. This leads to a reliance on the resume and a tendency to approach the interview casually. The resulting complacency puts the manager at a great disadvantage with today's well-coached candidates.

This complacency can be reinforced by three more realities confronting experienced managers and professionals.

INTERVIEWING IS NOT SEEN AS A BASIC SKILL

Interviewing and hiring others is not viewed as a core skill (outside of the human resources function). Line managers have full-time jobs in their own disciplines, or in management, where they must analyze, develop, design, forecast, negotiate, plan, review, sell, etc. Interviewing is not a skill they draw on to earn their pay.

TIME CONSTRAINTS

With today's push on productivity, interviewing others may be viewed as an unwelcome interruption in a busy day and a very low-priority activity. As Tom Jackson says in *Guerrilla Tactics in the Job Market*, "The employer hopes you are [the right one] so he can give up interviewing and get back to work."

NO INDIVIDUAL ACCOUNTABILITY

Increasingly, candidates are asked to come in for one or more rounds of interviews with many different people in the organization. The scheduling of 8–10 interviews for a single candidate may become a corporate strategy to syndicate the risk of hiring someone new.

"Don't blame *me* for hiring Charlie (who is not working out)— what about the other ten people who interviewed him?"

In truth, no one really *interviewed* the person. They all just "talked to Charlie." Personal accountability is therefore low.

Direct feedback within the organization about one's skill as an interviewer is rare. And we all know that candidates never tell those who interview them that they lack skills in this area.

Lack of accountability and the absence of critical feedback encourage the assumption that interviewing is a marginal activity at best and one's current skills are just fine.

While it's easy for experienced interviewers to be complacent about their current skill level in this area, it's dangerous to remain so.

READY-FOR-PRIME-TIME CANDIDATES

Candidates are competing aggressively for good jobs and are ready to pounce on the initiative in an interview. Their attitude toward any given interview is just the opposite of that of a busy manager who views the interview as an interruption in a busy day. To the candidate, it is the high point of the day—perhaps even the week—and certainly an important event worth preparing for. This vast difference in the way the candidate and the manager perceive the importance of the interview has helped shift the interviewing advantage from the complacent manager to the well-prepared candidate.

Time pressures on today's busy managers reinforce their loss of the advantage in an interview. Imagine for a minute these brief scenarios of two men getting ready for an interview today at 10:30. Peter is the hiring manager; Paul, the candidate.

As you read these, try to decide who has the advantage for the interview in terms of physical, emotional, and psychological preparation.

First, the interviewer, Peter.

Peter gets up at 6:30, gets dressed, breaks a shoelace, replaces it with one from another shoe, gulps down breakfast, pulls out into prime rush-hour traffic, gets a half mile from his office and finds that a broken traffic light makes him ten minutes late for an important 8 a.m. staff meeting with his boss to review fiscal year budgets.

The meeting ends at 9:30 and everyone is asked to submit a further 12 percent cut in their budgets by the end of the day. Peter's boss also asks him to stop by his office at 4:00 for a separate discussion "between the two of them." Peter's concentration at this point is not on his 10:30 interview.

After the staff meeting ends, Peter has two people waiting to see him and five phone calls to return. Although his employment manager sent him Paul's resume three days ago, Peter hasn't had a chance to look at it since then. Peter's second meeting of the morning ends at 10:40, at which time his secretary informs him that the candidate has been waiting for 20 minutes—is Peter ready for his interview?

Sound familiar?

Well, how about the candidate's day? Let's consider Paul's preparation for this same 10:30 interview.

He gets up at 8 a.m., not 6:30.

He has a relaxing breakfast and reads *The Wall Street Journal* and the business section of his local newspaper.

Paul goes to the closet and takes out a freshly pressed suit and just-shined pair of shoes. He spends a quiet half hour reviewing notes he has prepared over the last ten days for this interview with Peter's company.

Paul leaves home at 9:30—after the rush-hour traffic subsides. He arrives at 10:15, parks his car, and walks in at 10:20—ten minutes early for his 10:30 appointment.

Who do you think has the preparations advantage for this interview?

Help for the job seeker is plentiful. It can begin with Tom Jackson's book *The Perfect Resume*. New job seekers, or those with rusty skills, may prepare for the interview with another book: *Sweaty Palms: The Neglected Art of Being Interviewed* by H. Anthony Medley. Candidates with more experience may study books like *Guerrilla Tactics in the Job Market* by Tom Jackson or Theodore Pettus's *One on One: Win the Interview, Win the Job.*

Just the titles of these books should begin to shake the complacency of experienced interviewers who have not been trained or recently coached to fine-tune their skills. In the Pettus book, candidates are reminded of President Reagan's preparation for a press conference and are advised to spend up to one hour preparing an answer for each of several typical questions such as "Why do you want to change fields?" Those who take his advice seriously will spend far more time preparing their answer to one expected question than virtually any manager will spend preparing for the entire interview.

SUMMARY

When untrained and complacent interviewers interview well-prepared candidates they face an enormous challenge: getting behind the resume and really interviewing today's candidates.

The need identified in the Introduction—to predict future on-the-job behavior on the basis of an effective interview—has never gone away. The challenge today is to acquire and fine-tune the skills that will keep the advantage where it properly belongs in this process—with the interviewer.

2

Mistakes Interviewers Make

If he'll talk about himself, egg him on. As a rule, try to listen twice as much as you talk.*

Ted Pettus
One on One: Win the Interview, Win the Job

Experienced managers and professionals repeat the same interviewing mistakes year after year. This is an understandable outcome of the realities covered in Chapter 1: most managers have never been formally trained in effective techniques; interviewing is not a mainstream activity in their current job; and virtually no critique or feedback is provided about one's skills in this area. As a result, mistakes can go unnoticed and be repeated indefinitely. This chapter will show you some wrong turns an interview can take. Some of the detours may sound familiar.

---

*Theodore Pettus, *One on One: Win the Interview, Win the Job* (New York: Random House, 1979).

THE CHATTERBOX SYNDROME

Ted Pettus suggests the most common mistake interviewers make is talking too much. Several things foster this.

Most people who interview and hire others for their organization tend to be outgoing, personable, and generally good conversationalists. They have good verbal skills, and they enjoy using them. In their day-to-day supervision, coaching, or managing on the job, it is natural for them to do most of the talking.

Further, busy managers may not have time to adequately prepare for an interview, so they find it easy to start it off by talking about the job, the company, or their work. This is also viewed by some as an effective device to relax the candidate.

The difficulty with this approach is that interviewers don't know when to stop. One of the first subjects they talk about is the open job (if they are not talking about themselves). This is a dangerous area to get into deeply in the first part of the interview. Interviewers who give away a lot of critical information early in the interview may invalidate what they subsequently hear from the candidate.

The remedy for talking too much in an interview is to listen 80 percent of the time. Contrast this with Pettus's advice to job seekers in *One on One*: "Most of us talk too much. As a rule, try to listen twice as much as you talk." If candidates come in for interviews determined to listen 67 percent of the time, it will be hard for you to listen 80 percent of the time if you don't consciously plan to do so.

Some outplacement firms will counsel the fired executives they work with to "try to get the hiring manager to do all the talking. He or she will think you are very bright and very interesting." This advice to the job candidates to use the 80/20 listening rule on their terms, not yours, points out the key role of the listener in an interview.

Consider this advice H. Anthony Medley gives job seekers in his book *Sweaty Palms: The Neglected Art of Being Interviewed*: "Some interviewers will tell you something about the job before they start questioning you. Therefore, if you can easily segue into questioning him about the position early on, he may give you some valuable keys that you can use to guide the rest of the interview and create in him the realization that you are the right person to fill the position."

In *Guerrilla Tactics in the Job Market*, Tom Jackson provides the reader with 78 specific tactics. Tactic 69 advises, "At the beginning of each interview (particularly interviews based upon unadvertised jobs), after the formalities, ask the recruiter this question: 'Could you tell me in your own words what you are looking for in this position?' and then listen."

Despite the best intentions, even the most experienced interviewer will find it hard to resist this statement from a candidate early in the interview: "I've heard a lot about your company. Tell me— what's it like to work here?" Your response should be "I'll be glad to tell you about that later, but at this point I'd like to learn more about you."

If this ploy is not avoided, after the interviewer is finished talking about what it's like to work in the company the next question he or she hears may be "I see, and how long have you been here?" Pettus provides other questions for applicants to ask: "What were his own interviewing experiences when he was looking for a job? Did he ever imagine way back when that he would ever be so successful?"

Soon, the interviewer is doing all the talking. It may feel great, but nothing is being learned about the candidate.

This advice on listening applies to the beginning and middle portions of the interview, when you are evaluating the candidate. In the final stages of the interview—or during a call-back interview— when you are answering the candidate's questions and perhaps selling him on your organization, you will be doing most of the talking.

YOU DON'T SAY . . . OR DO YOU?

Another common mistake occurs when you are asking questions. It is something Tom Jackson calls the "telegraph":

"Very often interviewers will clearly show what they are looking for by the way they ask questions. 'You wouldn't mind doing some traveling, would you?' is a sample of a question that 'telegraphs' the answer. There are many such questions, and if you keep your listening apparatus tuned in you will pick up many clues to what traits are being sought."

The most common cause of this mistake is careless (or lazy) phrasing of questions. It is likely that you are about to telegraph the answer to your question if you start with a phrase like "Would you . . .," "Can you . . .," or "Do you. . . ." Some examples:

Would you say you are good with numbers?

Would you say you have good writing skills?

Would you describe yourself as a leader?

Can you accept criticism easily?

Do you think you'll enjoy living in Philadelphia?

Corporate information can also be telegraphed to a candidate when everyone on an interview schedule tends to ask the same question. "Will it bother you to work in an industry going through deregulation?" "Can you handle all the change our company is going through, even if you might not have the same boss two months from now?"

I DON'T KNOW WHY, I JUST LIKE THE GUY

Another mistake that can plague even an experienced interviewer is to jump to conclusions about a person. Carl Menk, president of an executive search firm in New York, commented on this in *Forbes* magazine: "It's been our experience that clients tend to make 80% of their decisions in the first 15 minutes of a meeting. The remaining hour or two is spent in confirming what they decided in those first 15 minutes."

Tom Jackson reports in *Guerrilla Tactics* of videotaped interviews where "[W]e saw employer representatives appear to make up their minds within the first five or ten minutes and then, throughout the balance of the interview, ask questions which would produce answers to justify the decision already reached."

The mistake of jumping to a conclusion can occur in three different ways. One, a "halo effect" sets in early in the process. We are positively disposed toward a candidate before we even meet him or her based just on the resume and the comments of others. When the person actually walks in, we begin to solidify that impression. If we like what we see, and the answers to our first few questions are positive, we begin to assume the person is good at everything. This "halo effect" sets in, and we ascribe positive qualities to the candidate with absolutely no evidence. "He's had good marketing experience, so *he's probably good at strategic planning, too*."

>>>**TILTED HALO** → On the other hand, if the candidate went to a school we're not impressed with, or we think the person is not attractive, we may decide he or she is not good at anything. If we are negatively impressed by someone, we may allow our conclusions to keep us from finding out further information that could possibly dispel those first impressions.

Second, we can jump to conclusions when we forget that everyone has strengths and limitations. Interviewers who conclude an interview without finding any negatives should not assume they've found the perfect candidate. Instead, they probably have not probed deeply enough during their interview with the candidate.

Finally, it's easy to jump to a conclusion if we assume the first explanation we hear for some behavior or accomplishment is the right one, or the only one. If we hear that someone finished a major project by working day and night for a week, we may assume he or she is a hard worker. However, further probing might reveal the person is a poor planner or simply fails to delegate.

UNFINISHED HOMEWORK

Also, it's a mistake to start an interview without knowing the right things about what the job requires. Interviewers tend to define what they are looking for in terms of who previously filled the job. Or, they believe a job description tells them what the job requirements are and this is all they need for interviewing.

When job descriptions provide answers to *what* questions only, and not to *how* questions, it's likely the interviewer is not really ready to conduct a revealing interview. The *what* of a job tells only what the person will do or what qualifications they need (e.g., 8–10 years of production experience or an MBA). The *how* of the job describes how the person must behave or perform to do the job (e.g., handle stress well, think strategically, have tireless energy, enjoy problem solving).

Interviewers must prepare for an interview by knowing their organization's culture and assessing the situational influences on the job. Then they'll understand what's required to do the job and what to look for in an interview.

FOLLOWING THE CANDIDATE'S SCRIPT

The next mistake involves improperly using the resume—either relying on it too much in the interview or assuming it is an accurate description of someone.

Many interviewers use the candidate's resume as a prop to conduct the interview. "I see you worked at United. How did you like working for them?" "I note that you graduated from the state university and majored in business. Did you enjoy your major?" In such an interview, little is learned about the candidate other than the information made obvious by the resume. This is a very serious mistake. When interviewers do not get behind the resume, they have no basis to predict on-the-job behavior. They have failed to separate the *what* about the candidate (he has an MBA; she has seven years of semiconductor design experience) from the *how* (he is intuitive; she is inexhaustible).

Further, resumes themselves can be misleading. Today's candidates have access to many resume preparation guides and services, some of which give very solid advice. Tom Jackson's *The Perfect Resume* promises readers: "By going through the perfect resume process we've outlined, you will have a resume equal to those of the top 10 percent of all job seekers."*

---

*Tom Jackson, *The Perfect Resume* (New York: Doubleday & Co., 1981).

Interviewers who are overly impressed with resumes, or who don't get behind them, may be hiring people who aren't as good as their resumes suggest. *Personnel Administrator* magazine reported in June 1986 on a survey of 100 companies, where "sixty-nine percent of the respondents suggested that resume preparation guides and resume preparation services advise, prompt or otherwise encourage people who are seeking jobs to embellish and fabricate information relating to their work history and/or academic profile."*

ENDINGS THAT COME TOO SOON

The final mistake interviewers make is to conclude the process when they are still not ready to predict on-the-job behavior. They decide whether or not they like the person. They have lots of facts and feelings, but no useful method or means by which they can confidently forecast how the person will perform if hired. This mistake denies them the kind of information about a candidate that will help them make a good hiring decision.

SUMMARY

Complacency and common mistakes may conspire to prevent exceptional interviewing. A sound method and practical techniques are needed to conduct revealing interviews.

---

*Richard D. Broussard and Dalton E. Brannen, "Credential Distortions: Personnel Practitioners Give Their Views." Reprinted from the June 1986 issue of *Personnel Administrator*, copyright 1986, The American Society for Personnel Administration, 606 North Washington Street, Alexandria, VA 22314, $40 per year.

3

Getting Behind the Resume

No two people have the same configuration of strengths and weaknesses.*

Peter Drucker
Management Tasks, Responsibilities, and Practice

R esumes list job candidates' experience and education. If this were all you need to know about a candidate, you could hire from the resume without ever conducting an interview. The reason you interview is to get *behind* the resume and see what the person is really like.

Complacency about one's effectiveness as an interviewer may be shattered when you consider what the career counselors are telling candidates. Here's what Ted Pettus has to say in *One on One*:

Men and women who conduct large numbers of interviews invariably develop their own interviewing format which they apply universally to one and all. This format is usually laced with various questions, techniques and idiosyncrasies which they have developed and polished over the years. Many interviewers

---

*Peter F. Drucker, *Management Tasks, Responsibilities, and Practice* (New York: Harper and Row, 1973).

defend this standardized interviewing as a method of maintaining objectivity from one applicant to another. I have long been convinced that laziness is their real motive.*

Whether the use of a standardized interview format is due to laziness or just bad habits, many interviewers may never get behind resumes with an effective method that illuminates *how* candidates did what they did.

Interviews that reveal only the "what" about a person are really just fact-gathering expeditions. The information gained is usually an array of facts about the candidate's education and experience—the resume factor—and, while a great deal of data has been collected, the interviewer still has no basis for predicting on-the-job behavior.

Peformance factors, the key predictors of ability and success, are not listed on a resume. They must be identified and confirmed through behavioral interviewing. This chapter describes a simple way to organize your approach to finding out what's important about a candidate.

MAJOR FACTORS TO CONSIDER

You could probably generate several hundred words or phrases to describe all the factors of experience and ability that might be required in a particular job (e.g., team player, self-starter, high energy, five years relevant experience, articulate). Such a list, to be helpful in the selection process, requires focus. For interviewing and evaluating purposes, attributes such as those listed above can be grouped into four major factor areas: the *Resume Factor* (education and experience), and the three *Performance Factors* (intellectual, interpersonal, and motivational). These factor groups can be used as the windows through which you view the range of attributes needed on the job and desired in a candidate.

When you organize your approach to evaluating a candidate's qualities in this manner, you will find it easier to cover what's important in the interview. You will also find that there is a common language for describing and comparing several candidates and for relating candidates to jobs.

---

*Theodore Pettus, *One on One: Win the Interview, Win the Job* (New York: Random House, 1979).

The principal things you need to learn about candidates are *what* they did (Resume Factor) and *how* they did it (Performance Factors). Behavioral interviewing draws out repeated samples of behavior so the interviewer has a basis for discovering *how* a person will do a job: how he or she approaches tasks, works with people, solves problems, and handles difficult situations. This approach also reveals the candidate's values, beliefs, goals, and interests and helps the interviewer more accurately predict future job performance.

BEHAVIORAL INTERVIEWING: NOT "JUST THE FACTS"

When you interview to understand behavior, you go far beyond focusing on the obvious qualities of education and experience that people present about themselves on their resume and in an interview. Behavioral interviewing allows the interviewer to observe and gather data about the candidate's intellectual, interpersonal, and motivational skills as well—factors that help predict the candidate's on-the-job performance in your company. These factors must be assessed in an employment interview to minimize the risk of making the wrong hiring decision. It is especially important to assess these factors with candidates who "look good on paper," that is, those who have impressive resumes.

Behavioral interviewing works because it draws people out. It can be likened to a technique Tom Peters describes in his 1985 book, *A Passion for Excellence*, as "naive listening"—the willingness and ability to listen without preconceptions. When applied in the interview, naive listening can help the interviewer uncover a number of premises about the candidate's behavior. Behavioral interviewing encourages candidates to talk about themselves in many different ways. Questions from the interviewer that begin with statements like "Tell me about . . ." encourage an elaborative response. An interviewer who uses such questions, and then sits back to listen for about 80 percent of the time, will discover a great deal about a candidate.

Behavioral interviewing is based on a widely recognized principle that past behavior is one of the best predictors of future behavior.

Therefore, the more samples gathered of past behavior, the greater likelihood of accurately predicting future behavior.

People develop values and beliefs early in life and, as adults, reflect them in their behavior. Beliefs drive behaviors. To conduct a revealing interview, you should draw out many samples of behavior from the candidate's background.

A major reason for conducting behavioral interviews is that job candidates do not change fundamentally after you hire them. You should imagine each candidate sitting before you holding a sign that reads: "My temperament and character are already formed. They will not change to fit your culture." Given this reality, your job as an interviewer is to discover the candidate's beliefs and resulting behavior, then decide whether this person will fit your organization.

Behavioral interviewing gets you tuned into explanations of what makes people tick rather than merely gathering facts on what they did.

WHERE THE BEHAVIORAL INTERVIEW BEGINS

The *Resume Factor* is the first thing you consider when qualifying a person for a position. It plays a key role in the screening process. Nearly all jobs require certain experience or education, or both. We transmit these minimum requirements in our employment ads, such as these from *The Wall Street Journal*:

Chief Financial Officer—must have experience in financial planning and a marketing background.

Sales Engineer—requires minimum 5 years direct outside industrial sales experience plus an engineering degree.

VP Marketing—Should have a strong technical background and heavy OEM computer sales experience.

These qualifications are identical to what you see on a resume. Prospective candidates reading these ads can mentally review their own resumes to see if they qualify. When you receive such resumes, you can immediately sort those that match what you are looking for from those that don't. Once you've selected candidates from the resumes, you still know only *what* each one has done. You need to learn *how* they have done these things. This requires moving from the *Resume Factor* to the three *Performance Factors*. All four factor areas must be assessed to predict a candidate's future behavior.

Performance Factors give life and dimension to the education, experience, and accomplishments described on the resume. The performance factors enable you to distinguish among candidates who share similar (or even identical) Resume Factors. As an example, imagine you are considering three candidates for the sales engineer position described in *The Wall Street Journal* ad. Each has the requisite five years industrial sales experience. What you need to know now are the performance factors that meet the requirements for this job: factors that you will predetermine in preparing for the interview. These factors may include "bright" (intellectual), "persuasive" (interpersonal), or "enthusiastic" (motivation). Your task in the interview will be to determine which of the candidates has the performance factors you are looking for.

Because interviewers are so used to focusing on the resume during the interview, heavy emphasis is placed on education and experience in the hiring process. The following exercise, which we use in our interviewing seminars, creates an immediate awareness among participants of the importance played by the performance factors.

In a recent *Fortune* magazine article, "America's Most Wanted Managers,"* executive recruiters named the top men and women in each of ten industries they would seek as chief executives. For each individual profiled, three or four adjectives were used to sum up the special qualities the recruiters admired. We provide seminar participants with a sampling of these words (reprinted below) and ask them to assign each word to the appropriate factor area:

Factor Areas
Resume Factor:
Performance Factors:
    Intellectual:
    Interpersonal:
    Motivational:

---

*Roy Rowan, "America's Most Wanted Managers," *Fortune*, Feb. 3, 1986.

Qualities of the Most-Wanted Managers

Ambitious	Intuitive
Canny	Inexhaustible
Charismatic	Outgoing
Perceptive	Innovative
People-Sensitive	Goal-Oriented

The reader is invited to try this exercise.

What surprises the seminar participants is that *none* of these qualities fits under the Resume Factor. Each of these individuals described had the education and experience that enabled him or her to begin and advance a successful career, and many of the performance factors have been honed by further training and years on the job. But, when it came to identifying the qualities that set them apart from the thousands of other executives in America, the words that were chosen can be categorized in these factor areas:

Resume Factor: None
Performance Factors:
    Intellectual: canny, perceptive, intuitive, innovative
    Interpersonal: charismatic, outgoing, people-sensitive
    Motivational: ambitious, goal-oriented, inexhaustible

This short exercise points up a key idea important to consider when interviewing candidates: what distinguishes good candidates from terrific ones will probably be found by exploring the Performance Factors rather than the Resume Factor.

Another example of success attributed to the Performance Factors appeared in *Money* magazine several years ago. Jane Evans, who is now President and CEO of Monet Crystal Brands, Inc. (and among the second ten "most wanted managers" identified by *Fortune*) was asked to explain her success. The then-Vice President of General Mills' fashion group credited her corporate climb to her "enormous energy, her sunny disposition and her inherent grasp of consumer marketing." "Enormous energy" is motivational, "sunny disposition" is interpersonal, and "inherent grasp of marketing" is intellectual. Nothing she stated about herself gave direct credit to her education and previous experience.*

---

*"Money Makers," *Money*, April 1983.

SUMMARY

Managers with exceptional interviewing skills move beyond the Resume Factor through effective behavioral interviewing. They use the Resume Factor as a starting point for assessing the full range of qualities a candidate will draw on for successful performance on the job. What follows in the next two chapters is an in-depth look at the Resume Factor and the Performance Factors. Knowledge of these factors, including a candidate's strengths and limitations in each, is essential for successful selection interviews.

4

The Resume Factor

If you survive the screening interview, it is generally an indication that your qualifications for the position are acceptable as far as the facts are concerned: you have enough experience and there is nothing on your resume . . . to disqualify you.*

H. Anthony Medley
Sweaty Palms: The Neglected Art of Being Interviewed

The Resume Factor includes education and experience. Some important dimensions of this factor are technical knowledge and experience, academic degrees, prior supervisory or management experience, and experience in a similar work environment or culture.

It is the factor used to begin the process of evaluating candidates for a specific position. Of the four factors to be considered, it is the most deceptive and misunderstood in terms of its role in interviewing.

Three challenges surround effective use of the Resume Factor when interviewing:

1. There is a tendency to overestimate the importance of certain credentials.

---

*H. Anthony Medley, *Sweaty Palms: The Neglected Art of Being Interviewed* (Berkeley, CA: Ten Speed Press, 1984).

2. Interviewers do not know how to offset limitations in the Resume Factor with strengths evidenced by the Performance Factors.

3. There is little understanding about how to use the Resume Factor to generate and confirm behavioral inferences about the candidate's Performance Factors.

Let's look at each of these challenges.

OVERESTIMATING CREDENTIALS

Organizations seek candidates with impressive credentials. Hiring managers will say, "Give me a 3.9 engineer from Stanford." Law firms admit, "If she is on Columbia's Law Review, we'll hire her." This attitude grows out of a recognition that people with such accomplishments have already gone through a number of tight screening procedures: admission to a top university, excellent grade point average selection for graduate or law school. The resulting assumption is that you don't have to probe their obvious abilities much further in the interview.

The difficulty with this approach is that those credentials alone do not necessarily explain how someone will perform in the future, nor do they separate one well-qualified candidate from another.

When reviewing the resume of an experienced candidate, use similar caution: experience does not necessarily correlate with ability. A person may be employed for some time and have a great deal of experience and yet be an average performer.

What we know about the Resume Factor is that, while it is our basic qualifying tool for candidates, it is *the factor least likely to predict on-the-job failure and poor performance*. People seldom are let go from jobs because they lack the right college degrees or haven't had the right experience. They are asked to leave organizations because of limitations in one or more of the Performance Factors: for example, they are not motivated, they do not get along with others, they have no curiosity about their jobs, or they are not interested in their work. It is therefore risky to place too much importance on just the Resume Factor.

Another important thing to remember is that the value of experience in the Resume Factor is derived from its relevance to your company and its culture. A candidate's success in one work setting may not necessarily predict success in your organization. In *The 100 Best Companies to Work for in America*, the authors give many examples of how corporate culture affects employee fit with an organization. At Intel, the California microelectronics giant, people work in a very confrontational environment. A successful career experience at Intel, or an unsuccessful one, must be assessed for its relevance to another company's environment: Would a candidate's confrontational style be an asset or liability in your company? Experience is relative.

OFFSETTING RESUME FACTOR LIMITATIONS

Learning how to use behavioral factors to offset shortcomings in specific experience is a major step in becoming a skilled interviewer. Organizations list exact experience requirements (e.g., five years direct sales experience) because a uniform approach makes the screening process easier. Those without five years experience are screened out early in the process. The problem, however, is that someone with only three or four years experience may be the best candidate.

We can presume that experience helps build performance factors such as wisdom, maturity, and commitment. The effective interviewer will look for evidence of these behavioral qualities throughout the interview, then use such evidence to compensate for a possible lack of certain experience. The effective interviewer will also use techniques to confirm inferences made about the candidate's behavioral qualities from the experience described on the resume.

USING THE RESUME FACTOR
TO EXPLORE PERFORMANCE FACTORS

The Resume Factor is a rich source of facts and data to use as the starting point for generating behavioral premises. By asking questions that have the candidate explain the *how* of *what* he or she has done, interviewers can explore the full range of behavioral qualities the candidate would bring to the job. Chapter 17, "The Self Appraisal Question," is entirely devoted to exploring this technique. It is important to remember that the Resume Factor is merely the starting point for conducting an effective interview.

THE ROLE OF THE RESUME IN THE INTERVIEW PROCESS

While the Resume Factor is essential in the assessment of all candidates, actual use of the resume *during* the interview should be kept to a minimum. Sometimes the resume becomes a prop for conducting the interview. When that happens, the interviewer goes down the resume, asking questions about facts that are already apparent. Because the interviewer never gets behind the resume, he or she tends to shift the entire interview emphasis onto this one factor. At the end of the session, the interviewer will know little more than what is on the resume. There are two other risks to using the resume during the interview.

Many of today's job candidates invest considerable energy in crafting an exceptional resume. If the entire interview is spent discussing what is on the resume, the interviewer is doing exactly what the candidate had planned: focusing on the resume, not the candidate.

Lastly, resumes may be written by professional services whose primary aim is to make the candidate look good, even at the cost of accuracy. *Personnel Administrator* magazine for June 1986 disclosed: "One study reported that 80 percent of the resumes investigated contained misleading information about employment histories, and approximately 30 percent either misrepresented or fabricated academic credentials."* Not all professional resume writing services are guilty of this, but these statistics indicate that interviewers should be aware of this problem.

---

*Reprinted from the June 1986 issue of *Personnel Administrator*, copyright 1986, The American Society for Personnel Administration, 606 North Washington Street, Alexandria, VA 22314, $40 per year.

SUMMARY

It is important to understand the proper role of the Resume Factor when you interview. Candidate resumes summarize this factor, but it is not necessary to have the resume in front of you during an interview to explore the Resume Factor. You can review the resume before the interview, and note significant topics, time periods, or accomplishments you want to cover. From that point on, the person's education and experience should serve as the basis for questions that will allow you to gather information about the three important Performance Factors.

5

The Performance Factors

*At H-P, a division general manager of a $75 million opera-tion will spend an hour or so with final candidates for a first-line purchasing job. Other interviewers include bosses at two or three levels, numerous peers and potential subor-dinates; each also spends an hour or more. They make the time. Moreover, each of the interviewers zeroes in on traits that most people would call mushy and immeasurable.**

Tom Peters
"Let Your Line Managers Do the Hiring"
San Jose Mercury News

THE INTELLECTUAL FACTOR

The first Performance Factor we will consider is the Intellectual Factor. From your own experience, you probably know that this is the toughest factor to measure in an interview. A glib and articulate candidate can mesmerize you into thinking he or she is extremely bright and quick. And some very bright people will be shy and reti-cent until they get to know you—which requires months, not just the time of an interview. This Performance Factor in particular under-scores the importance of getting behind the resume and using tech-niques that reveal as much as possible about the candidate.

*From Tom Peters, "On Excellence," as published in *San Jose Mercury News*, July 10, 1986. © 1986 TPG Communications.

There are three aspects of the Intellectual Factor that you will want to consider: Intellectual *capacity, application* of that capacity, and whether facts or feelings predominate in *decision making style.* One useful way to think about the Intellectual Factor in relation to interviewing is to consider how various intellectual traits are classified from simple to complex. One such stratification is provided by Benjamin S. Bloom in his book *Cognitive Domain.*

Bloom's sequential classification goes from *knowledge* (ability to memorize, recall, or repeat information) through the following hierarchy:

Comprehension—ability to interpret or restate information

Application—ability to use or apply information

Analysis—ability to divide complex knowledge into separate parts

Synthesis—ability to bring together separate elements of knowledge to form new patterns

Evaluation—ability to make judgments or appraisals based on knowledge or given criteria.

You can see immediately that the task of evaluating candidates calls for a high degree of intelligence! It uses the most complex intellectual process—evaluation. However, Bloom's classification of thinking behaviors also supports the importance of learning the multiple dimensions of the candidate's ability to apply his or her own intellectual capacity through the skills of analysis, synthesis, and evaluation. The questioning techniques presented in this book will help you explore this factor in candidates.

Capacity

Intellectual capacity is what people are born with, and it is what they draw on to solve problems. IQ tests are one way to measure intellectual capacity, but they can't be used in interviews. The lack of quantifiable data to measure a candidate's intellectual capacity is frustrating to many managers. Often they seek other kinds of quantitative measurements such as college or graduate school entrance tests (SAT and GRE, respectively), which score a person's verbal and mathematical aptitude using a 200 to 800 point range. Law firms have tended to give considerable weight to the LSAT scores, and some employers like to check an MBA's GMAT scores. The higher such scores, the quicker the manager's conclusion that this person is highly intelligent.

>>>**THE BAD NEWS** → Studies of test scores for admission to college or graduate school have established a correlation between high scores and good performance for only the first year or two of school. The National Association for Law Placement, a professional association that upholds standards for law schools and law firms in recruitment and hiring practices, reports a similar finding relative to LSAT scores: They have only been validated for correlation with first-year performance in law school.

In the autumn of 1985, the Harvard Business School dropped the GMAT test as a requirement for admission. In announcing this decision, Harvard stated that personal qualities are much more relevant than test scores in predicting success in business.

If test scores are not available, some interviewers will turn to school grades as evidence of the Intellectual Factor. But school grades, too, can be misleading. *The Wall Street Journal* recently reported on its study of major colleges and universities and their practice of awarding degrees with "distinction" (cum laude, magna cum laude, and summa cum laude). They reported that 75 percent of the graduates of Harvard College graduate with "distinction," while at Columbia the comparable percentage—which tends never to change from year to year—is only 15 percent!*

I have to admit my own bias as an interviewer. Before I read that article, if I was interviewing a man who was graduated from Harvard (but without "distinction") and a woman who was graduated cum laude from Columbia, I would not have known that the Harvard alumnus was in the *bottom 25 percent* of his class and that the Columbia graduate was in the *top 15 percent* of hers.

The use of test scores or degrees with distinction to establish the intellectual capacity of a candidate you are interviewing may not be a valid approach. (MIT, for example, does not grant any degrees

---

*As reported by Wendy L. Wall, "Summa Cum Blah: Some Colleges Seek to Lower the Laudes," *The Wall Street Journal*, April 14, 1983.

with distinction.) The most valid inferences about capacity will come from answers to questions that probe the application of that capacity.

Application

Even if you feel confident that a candidate's intellectual capacity is great, it won't be of use to your organization unless that individual uses it effectively. People who rely on shallow thinking or make snap judgments may not bring all of their thinking power to bear on the problems they have to solve. They many not be capable of developing workable solutions to complex problems.

To learn how candidates use and apply their intellectual capacity, look for clues during the interview. You can observe analytical ability when you give a candidate some specific problems to analyze. These can be situations you think he or she should have experienced in the past, or will be likely to experience in your organization. Pose a sample problem and ask applicants to tell you how they would handle it. This will begin to show you something about their analytical skills and problem-solving abilities. Pay attention to how well they organize their answers. How creative are they? How imaginative? Do their answers give you some evidence of their foresight and verbal skills? The problem situations you present for solution by the candidate can also help you determine the candidate's likely fit with your organization's culture. Has he solved similar problems elsewhere? Does his approach fit with the way your people solve problems? While problem-solving, does she analyze factors that are important in your organizational culture?

Effective questioning techniques are your most powerful way to measure use of intellectual capacity in an interview. By asking the right kinds of questions, you'll have a chance to see how a person approaches the intellectual tasks that are important to the job.

One of our clients does financial trading, which requires employees to have skill with numbers and be quick thinkers. A favorite question of a senior trader involves a two-part probe:

Q.—Are you good with numbers?
A.—Yes.
Q.—OK, how much is 12×24?

The answer (288) is not the most important part of the response. What this interviewer looks for is how the candidate arrives at the answer. If the applicant used one of two mental short-cuts ($12 \times 12 \times 2$ or 24×10 plus 2×24) it's all right. However, if the person had to think: "24×12? Let's see. Two times four is eight, two times two is four ...," then the answer is evidence to this senior trader that the person is not good with numbers.

Decision Making Style

The third aspect of the Intellectual Factor is how decisions are made. We all use a combination of both facts and feelings in our decision making. Engineers, controllers, and lawyers are among those whose work decisions must rely heavily on facts. Advertising copywriters, designers, and many sales people may rely principally on interpretations based on feelings or intuition. However, controllers also use intuition, for example, to assess the mood of an outside auditor, and lawyers respond to their feelings when they "read" a jury. Advertising copywriters must carefully count seconds and words to decide where to cut a "shoot" into a 30-second commercial, and sales people must use product facts and terms of sale to close a deal.

When assessing the Intellectual Factor, you may be concerned that the candidate overuses either facts or feelings to make decisions. If you feel the use of facts is too high, you can inquire about important people decisions the candidate has made and how the decisions were reached. If your concern is overreliance on feelings, ask about the process the candidate uses for making important decisions or how he or she reacts to people who rely just on the facts at hand to make a decision. Other questions to probe this aspect of the Intellectual Factor are provided in the appendix.

The Intellectual Factor is difficult to evaluate in the interview, but it is extremely important to assess. To gather information about the three dimensions of the Intellectual Factor, you must use certain questioning techniques and conduct the interview in such a way that repeated evidence about this factor will be generated.

THE INTERPERSONAL FACTOR

The second Performance Factor is the Interpersonal Factor. This factor helps predict the way people will influence others and interact with those they work with. It is important to assess this factor accurately. Effective interviewers do this by having candidates describe past behavior in many different situations.

Interviewers who make their assessment in this area based on the candidate's behavior *during* the interview may not have the evidence they need to make a correct judgment. The applicant's appearance, manner, and demeanor may lead an interviewer to reach certain conclusions about the candidate based on what is only a fragmentary representation of the Interpersonal Factor.

There are many dimensions to the Interpersonal Factor. The most easily observed are those you are likely to infer from the candidate's actions during the interview: e.g., he or she appears to be friendly, self-confident, outgoing, and assertive. The more complex traits—ability to be a team player, diligence, maturity, flexibility—are not easily determined by mere observation. Evidence of these qualities can be gained only by having the candidate relate many instances of previous behavior.

To be successful on the job, people draw on a wide range of talents and abilities, many of which are interpersonal. Most of these interpersonal qualities can be classified into four different personality types or traits. Such classifications date back all the way to Hippocrates, figured prominently in the theories of psychologist Carl Jung, and are still in use today.

The profile grouping system we use was developed by Professional Dynametric Programs, Inc. (PDP) of Woodland Park, Colorado. The four traits used to analyze behavior are:

Dominance (e.g., aggressiveness, competitiveness, perseverance);

Extroversion (e.g., friendliness, personableness, ability to work as part of a team);

Pace (e.g., easygoing, cooperative, unhurried attitude);

Conformity (e.g., systematic, methodical, rules-oriented approach).

Each of these traits is found to some degree in everyone, and most people have one trait that is much stronger than the others. What is important for our purposes in selection interviewing is that 50 to 70 percent of a person's on-the-job performance is explained by his or her strongest trait.

>>>**THE PEOPLE BEHIND THE TRAITS** → It may be easier to understand these trait descriptions if you visualize them in terms of certain shoppers you may have encountered at the supermarket: the *dominant* one barges into the express checkout line with 15 items and a check to cash, ignoring the signs indicating nine items or less and no checks; the *extrovert* talks with friends in every aisle and with the butcher and checkout clerk; the *easy-going, unhurried* shopper urges people behind him to go ahead, even when there's only a small difference in the number of items they're buying; the *conformist* enters the store equipped with a shopping list and discount coupons organized by aisle.

One of these four aspects of the Interpersonal Factor—dominance—is probably very relevant to the success of Lee Iacocca, president of the Chrysler Corporation. Interviewing Iacocca about his best-selling 1984 autobiography, *Newsweek* asked him, "What is the lesson of this book?" Iacocca responded, "I think it is that if I keep working at this and want it bad enough, I can have it. It's called perseverance."

Perseverance is a key characteristic of persons with high dominance. In the book, Iacocca gave another example of his perseverance, indicating this is probably a quality he has evidenced throughout his life. When he was an undergraduate at Lehigh University, he was concerned about a required course in statistics. Many of his fellow engineers would stay up late Friday night drinking beer and would never make it to this 8 a.m. Saturday class. Iacocca always showed up, and he earned an A in the course. "I guess I had perseverance," he said about himself. This key factor in his present success was evident when he started college and is something he has no doubt drawn on throughout his life. Specific questions for exploring any of the four aspects of the Interpersonal Factor are given in the appendix.

To accurately assess the Interpersonal Factor, more evidence is needed than the interviewer's observation of the candidate during the interview. Again, the more complex aspects of a person's interpersonal skills—flexibility, maturity, ability to work with a team—are best determined by gathering many examples of how the candidate has performed in the past. Behavioral interviewing will help you interpret this factor correctly.

THE MOTIVATIONAL FACTOR

Motivation, the third Performance Factor, is a very key factor in the assessment of today's candidates. As you understand this factor, you will begin to read whether the person you're considering hiring will stay on the job and find the work satisfying—and how much effort he or she will give to it. Motivation is more than the degree to which a person is a "hard worker." In fact, "hard work" is something you can't probe for directly in an interview—to the lazy person, everything is hard work. To understand this factor, you have to understand all its dimensions.

Successful people in any business tend to really like what they're doing—which is what motivates them to do it well. There are four indicators of motivation you should look for when you interview candidates: their *goals*, their *interests*, their *drive or energy level*, and finally, their *mobility*.

Goals

Ask candidates about their goals, and you're likely to get a rehearsed answer. Most candidates for a job know either through their own experience (or through coaching from a placement director or job counselor) that when you go for an interview you should be ready to answer, "What are your goals?" or "Where do you want to be in five years?"

Even if candidates tend to come in with prepared answers, you should question them about their goals. They may describe their goals in a way that suggests a clear career path, but this is no guarantee they are *actually* committed to such objectives. So how do you, as an interviewer, check their goals for validity? One way is to ask candidates, "Why have you picked this particular goal? And what makes you so sure it's right for you?" Those who are committed to their goals will be able to tell you—and in very specific terms—why the objectives they just outlined are personally relevant. For the genuinely motivated, goals will relate to what they know about themselves, about their strengths and interests. If they give you only a shallow response to this question (e.g., "Actually I'm pretty flexible on what I want to be."), then you may have a caution flag on their motivation. They may simply have memorized a clever-sounding goal and may not be really committed to it.

When people talk about goals, another thing to listen for is whether they link goal statements to promotions and titles—or whether they talk about achieving excellence and learning what's needed to do the job effectively. This distinction is particularly important among younger people who still have a lot to learn. Their statements ought to reflect these kinds of goals.

Some evidence about the importance of commitment to goals comes from a study done by Dr. Charles A. Garfield, Ph.D., and the Performance Sciences Corporation in Palo Alto, California. After measuring the performance of 1,500 high-achieving professionals, they found the *best predictor* of long-range success was "commitment to a well-articulated mission accompanied by well-defined goals."[*] Consider your own experience: Successful people you know in business or the professions, in politics or sports, probably all know what they want to do and are really committed to doing it. So when you run into job candidates who are not committed or do not have clear goals, you may have justifiable concerns about their Motivation Factor.

Goals are important, but they are only one element of the motivation factor; the next aspect you should look at is *interests.*

Interests

When people do things they like, their motivation is heightened. To know how motivated they will be, you need to understand their interests. If there's a high correlation between what people like and what your job offers, you can predict with better odds that they will be satisfied and stay at the job.

---

[*]By permission of Charles A. Garfield, Ph.D., Performance Sciences Corp., Palo Alto, CA, 1983.

The 100 Best Companies to Work for in America describes the major plus of working for the 3M Company this way: "It's a good place for people who *like* to tinker with ideas." Apply this principle to your own situation—there are probably parts of your job that you don't like as well as others—and chances are that you tend to postpone them to the end of the day, the end of the week, or even the end of the decade! If you're a "morning person," you probably don't get up to tackle that part of the job that least interests you; you finish the part that's of greatest interest first.

A number of studies tried to correlate performance in the Harvard Business School with later success in the business world. They found virtually no correlation between success in business and performance in the *first* year at the Harvard Business School. There is, however, a reasonably high correlation between performance in the *second* year of the business school and later success in business.

The major difference between the first and second years at the Harvard Business School is that during the first year, virtually all the courses are required. There are no electives, no choice about what you're going to study. But in the second year, virtually all the courses are electives, and the students can pick the courses they are interested in.

The point is that when you can see how well people do in an activity in which they're interested, then you have a basis on which to predict future performance. Since there is such a high correlation betweeen interest and performance, you have to measure interest level. In addition, highly motivated people who are interested in what they do tend to become self-starters. As the individual obtains more seniority in a company, this quality grows in importance, because the higher you go, the more generalized the directions from above become. At senior levels, managers tend to get fairly vague instructions like, "Get us into this market," or "Find a way to increase volume," or "Let's see if we can reduce costs next year." When people receive these undefined but critical goals from management—stating *what* but not *how*—they must be deeply interested in what they are doing in order to successfully accomplish them.

Sometimes you find people who are not really interested in their work. Perhaps you've had a conversation like the following with a clerk or a secretary: "Have you finished the Smith report?" you ask.

"No, I was waiting to speak to you."

"What about giving it a try on your own?"

"I never thought of that."

This conversation probably takes place between a manager and an employee who is not very interested in what he or she is doing. Such people never think about the job until you speak to them, have a low interest in their work, are not highly motivated, and are probably not very productive.

Drive

The third dimension of the Motivational Factor is drive. You will get a reading on this aspect of motivation by gathering evidence about the energy level of the candidates you interview. Energy helps get people through day-to-day frustrations they encounter on the job, and over other obstacles as well. It can also result in high work capacity, especially if employees focus drive and energy on the job, not just on sports or outside pursuits. Playing racquetball or bowling four nights a week may demonstrate high energy and contribute to a higher overall energy capacity. However, if people exhaust themselves with these activities and there is no energy left over for the job, their energy won't be very useful to your organization. What is essential to assess is drive and energy that relate to performance on the job.

There are two ways to consider energy—the amount people have and the way they apply it most effectively. You are probably asking yourself, "How on earth can I measure someone's energy in an interview?" One way is to ask the person you're interviewing to describe a typical day.

When you ask this question, a candidate may answer, "Well, no day is typical." In that case, ask the candidate to describe yesterday—"What happened from the time you got up in the morning to the time you went to bed last night? Describe what happened all day long."

A favorite example, although a bit extreme, comes from a write-up about Phil Beekman, who joined Seagram's Corporation as president after running a division of Colgate-Palmolive. He was quoted as saying, "I set highly ambitious goals for myself and everyone under me, but I'm not asking anyone to work any harder than myself." According to the article, he arrives at the office by 7 a.m. and often has meetings in the evening. Before he even arrives at work he jogs five miles or more each morning.

Now *there's* a person who has considerable drive and high energy! He can handle a range of matters throughout a full day and bring a lot of drive and energy to all he does.

Here's another example, from a *Wall Street Journal* article about a union organizer named George Hudspeth:

> Mr. Hudspeth's day begins at 7 a.m. with a 15-second breakfast that consists of a half a glass of milk and a fistful of vitamins. The day often ends, as one did recently, at 11:30 p.m. when Mr. Hudspeth, standing in his shorts in his kitchen, calls a political ally on a local zoning commission to map strategy.*

Typically, people with high energy can do a normal day's work and then some or still carry on many spare-time activities without undue fatigue. You should be alert to candidates who lack drive or have low energy levels, particularly if you believe it will affect their career potential in the position you're trying to fill. People with above-average energy typically have the capacity to take on more responsibility and extra duties. They can grow with the job, and their drive helps to carry them past the frustrations that are found in any job.

>>**OF ROCKETS AND RAILROADS** → The type of energy a person displays is identifiable by the way it's applied: Some individuals have the capacity for concentrated bursts of energy directed at a specific task or deadline; others can sustain their energy output across everything they do. We can liken the first type of energy to a rocket; the second type is more like a locomotive. One way to view the differences between these two energy types is to think of a sprinter (rocket) and a marathon runner (locomotive). People whose energy is more akin to a rocket are well-suited for project work, where deadlines may require very concentrated periods of work. They may be ideal as design engineers, merchandising managers, loan officers, or trial attorneys. Those who apply their energy evenly across all that they do may do well as

---

*David Wessel, "Pitchman for Labor," *The Wall Street Journal*, August 22, 1986.

front desk managers, financial traders, quality control technicians, or tax and estate lawyers.

People whose type of energy is wrong for the job you place them in will burn up a great deal of their available energy trying to adjust to the job. This drains the total amount of energy they have available and gives them less to apply to their assigned work.

Mobility

Our society has become more mobile. However, changing values and the workplace demographics of dual-career families make the question of mobility one of growing significance when assessing motivation. This question of mobility becomes extremely important when you are considering a candidate who must relocate in order to accept the job.

However, you should be cautious about EEO concerns when probing the mobility factor (see Chapter 19). Executive search professionals have a special interest in exploring a candidate's mobility because they often source candidates who must relocate. Gordon Wahls of Philadelphia has developed a series of questions that raise the issues that affect executive mobility. He asks candidates to declare what the impediments are to their relocation by considering the following questions:

- Where were you (and your spouse) born?
- Where did you (both) grow up?
- Where do (both) your parents live now?
- What is the state of (both) your parents' health?
- What are the ages of your children? Are any in their junior or senior year of high school?
- Do any of your children benefit from special education?
- Does your spouse work? How likely is it that he or she can find a suitable new job?

To avoid telegraphing answers to these questions, Gordon Wahls suggests telling the candidate that there will be seven questions and to listen to all of them before answering any. The one the person chooses to answer first can be very telling about his or her major concern and true mobility. (An interesting interviewing technique, regardless of the subject matter!)

MOTIVATION AND SUCCESS ON THE JOB

One of our clients has this "Prescription for Achieving Excellence" that reflects the work of Dr. Charles A. Garfield, Ph.D., and sums up the importance of motivation on the job:

Symptoms:
Feeling overworked?
Anxious about deadlines?
Concerned about not achieving excellence on a consistent basis?

Prescription:
Find something you love to do.
Work hard and work smart.
Focus on results.
Challenge yourself and learn from your mistakes.
Make movies in your mind.
Believe in yourself and take care of yourself.
Build support networks.

Excellence is achieved through consistency and teamwork

SUMMARY

Motivation is a key performance factor that can be assessed in a behavioral interview. When it and the other two Performance Factors, intellectual and interpersonal are considered, a revealing picture of the candidate's potential for success begins to emerge: you will know not only *what* they have done, but *how* they have done it. These factors are among the "mushy and immeasurable" traits that Tom Peters refers to in the article quoted at the beginning of this chapter. Successful interviewers will gather as much information about these traits as possible, because they are the factors that determine which candidates will succeed in the culture and on the job.

6

Corporate Culture
And the Hiring Process

Corporate cultural factors have a major effect on the attitudes and behavior of a company's employees.*

Terrence E. Deal and Allen A. Kennedy
Corporate Cultures

The hiring process really boils down to fitting people against jobs. To do this, you need a way to define both candidates and jobs in similar behavioral terms: *how* the work gets done as well as *what* gets done.

The Resume and Performance Factors (Chapters 4 and 5) describe the people side of the hiring equation in these terms. You also need a way to describe the job and the organization in a way that will help you hire the people that will be successful in your environment.

To gain a complete picture of what it takes to fit people to jobs, you need to be able to define your organization's culture, then put that into a useful candidate/job profile. The purpose of this chapter

---

*Terrence E. Deal and Allen A. Kennedy, *Corporate Cultures* (Reading, MA: Addison-Wesley, 1982).

and the next is to help interviewers define and use their organizational culture in the hiring process.

Corporate culture has been defined by Stanley Davis of the Boston University School of Management as "a pattern of beliefs and expectations shared by others. These values produce rules for behavior and pressure to conform on the job." The major business book of the 1980s, *In Search of Excellence,* tells us that "excellent companies are marked by very strong cultures, so strong that you either buy into their norms or get out. There's no halfway house for most people in the excellent companies."

A "GOOD CATCH" OR A FISH OUT OF WATER?

Employees who are excellent performers in one setting may not work out at all in another. The effort required for employees to adapt to a work environment where their approach, style, values, and behavior run counter to the culture can drain much of their available energy, leaving little for job-related tasks. Parallels from nature can be drawn. The high-altitude vision of an eagle or hawk is not necessary or useful in spotting prey on the floor of the Amazon jungle. Polar bears and penguins won't make it there, either. Out of their most suitable environment, these creatures struggle in even the most routine pursuit. It is the same with people.

DON'T HIRE A CANDIDATE WHO DOESN'T FIT IN

To be successful in any organization, employees must fit into the work culture. Interviewers must use techniques to assess a candidate's fit with their own company. It is essential to know how people will behave on the job and how their way of doing their work will mesh with the workplace culture. This approach to hiring reflects the growing recognition that corporate culture and candidate qualifications must fit reasonably well if employees are going to stay and achieve.

Fortune magazine pointed out in an article several years ago that it may be easier to change the personnel of a company than to change its culture. "In the long term, according to many human resource specialists, the key to culture is whom you hire and promote. People often get jobs and move up more for the degree to which they fit prevailing norms than for any objective reason."

For those who must interview and hire someone from outside their department, division, company, or even industry, this carries very important implications. They need to know if candidates will fit their culture.

Ztel, a high-tech start-up that filed for bankruptcy in 1985, is a company that found out the high price an organization pays for not fitting people to the company culture. Its failure was analyzed by *Business Week* shortly after Ztel filed for reorganization under Chapter 11:

> "Early on, however, Ztel made a key mistake. Instead of hiring an entrepreneur to run things, the founders recruited a management team more suited to a large company. "They didn't want to have to switch management as the company grew," says Gerald R. Birr, the former chief financial officer. In April 1983, Ztel lured Peter S. Anderson from Mohawk Data Sciences Corporation to become its president. Most other top officers also had little experience at startups.*

The *Business Week* article goes on to describe Anderson's style: "Unlike most presidents of small companies, Anderson managed at arm's length. He set up a formal structure and separate operating plans for each division, with little interaction among the units." According to Ztel's co-founder, Richard A. Epstein, Anderson was aloof: "I don't know how many times I asked Peter to come to the lab, but he stayed in his office. He wasn't that visible to the troops."

Two more examples illustrate the importance of "fit" in hiring.

The president of Microsoft, a company that develops software for personal computers, quit his job after only 11 months. As reported in *The Wall Street Journal:*

---

*Lois Therrien and Mark Maremont, "How Ztel Went from Riches to Rags," *Business Week*, June 17, 1985.

They were a company of programmers, really smart people. [Towne, the president] was brought in to turn it into a business. Mr. Towne's management style isn't believed to have suited the more freewheeling Microsoft.*

An example from *Fortune* magazine concerns Hewlett-Packard, where Paul Ely (now CEO of Convergent Technologies) was passed over for the number two job of chief operating officer and resigned from the company. The person selected in place of him, according to the April 1985 article, "... would do a better job inside the H-P culture than Ely. Ely was able but cocky. Within the parameters of H-P's culture, he was just in bounds."

KNOW YOUR CORPORATE CULTURE
(CANDIDATES PROBABLY DO)

Such stories are more common than reported and occur at all levels in all kinds of organizations. Despite the emphasis of today's business press on corporate culture, its impact on the people you hire too often gets overlooked. Careless or untrained interviewers may tell a candidate, "We place a high value in our company on customer service," and then lob a question on top of it:

"Would you say that is a high value for you, too?"

The candidate who wants the job will say, "Yes, I believe we must place the customers first and do our utmost to service their needs."

Clearly, this kind of interview will not assess a candidate's true fit with the organization. It is important for interviewers to understand their culture, but not to convey it through the questions they ask.

The concept of fitting candidates into cultures is powerfully illustrated in *The 100 Best Companies to Work for in America*. In their extensive research, the authors used a five-point rating system that yielded a list of companies that employees really like to work for. The companies were rated on pay, benefits, job security, chance to move

---

The Wall Street Journal, June 22, 1983.

up, and ambience. The latter three are especially reflective of key aspects of corporate culture. Relative to hiring, what is most relevant about this book is the pithy summary it provides of each company in terms of the one major plus and the one major negative about working there. Consider an example that speaks volumes about this critical fit of people with the corporate culture:

Goldman Sachs & Co. (major investment banking firm)
    Plus—If you like the money game, here's a good team to play on.
    Minus—If you like other games, you may not have time for them.*

A candidate reading this "minus" would infer that employees at Goldman Sachs work very long hours. Therefore, if an interviewer is to determine how successfully candidates will fit into the Goldman Sachs culture, high energy and the capacity to have a consuming interest in their work are the vital characteristics to seek out. Both energy and interest are motivational factors, and good interviewers must know techniques for finding out about these.

Another example from *The 100 Best Companies* is Intel (microelectronics). There, the researchers identified the following:

    Plus—A chance to be one of the best and the brightest.
    Minus—They yell at each other a lot.

For engineers and computer scientists at Intel, it's not enough to be on the cutting edge of technology. They must also be comfortable in a highly confrontational work environment, or they won't be successful. Interviewing for Intel thus requires an accurate reading of candidates' interpersonal qualities and the kind of environment in which they function most effectively.

Corporate cultures often vary *within* the same industry. Consider these summary statements for two major New York City banks whose world headquarters are only a few miles apart.

The Morgan Bank
    Plus—Probably the most prestigious bank in the country.
    Minus—You may not have enough money to open an account here.

---

*© 1984, 1985, Levering, Moskowitz & Katz, *The 100 Best Companies to Work for in America*, New American Library. Reprinted by arrangement with Addison-Wesley Publishing Company.

Citicorp

Plus—Plenty of action and highly charged people to work with.

Minus—If you don't like to take chances, you won't do well here.

These statements suggest that someone who may be successful at Morgan Bank may not fit Citicorp at all, and vice versa.

Interviewers who never get far beyond the Resume Factor may credit 10 years experience in one bank as evidence that the person can succeed in the other. There may be no basis for this conclusion, because the shared industry experience was gained in a very different work culture.

Company cultures also vary *across* industries. Consider this example from *New Age*, March 1985, in which the reader was advised:

Don't Bring Your Old Frame into the New Frame: "The worst mistake I made," Zenith Gross says, "was to carry my high-powered business-world mores into my relationships with editors and agents. In business, when you say 'I'll get back to you' it means before lunch. In publishing, it can mean before Christmas. In my old position, writing a memo was a way of life. But when I wrote my agent a long memo, she thought I was insulting her ability."

In spite of the enormous wave of books and articles on corporate culture, little has been written about how interviewers can use relevant aspects of their organization's culture to conduct effective interviews with external candidates. The literature for *candidates*, however, is full of vital information about what it's really like to work at a company. Today's candidates no longer have to try to "wing it" through an interview. They are well-prepared because they've studied your company or industry culture. They know what to say in an interview to convince the hiring manager that they'll fit right in.

Sometimes the candidate doesn't have to look very far for this information. Recently, in the employment office lobby of a major U.S. corporation, we observed dozens of new college graduates and young professionals waiting to be interviewed for an executive training program.

On the wall behind the receptionist's desk, greeting candidates as they arrived, was a poster that stated:

"We are . . .
  customer-focused,
  creative, can-do people who
  deliver on the bottom-line . . ."

By proudly proclaiming to its potential employees the kind of people they like to have in their organization, this company was giving interviewees an advantage. As we looked at the eager eyes of some of those in the room, it struck us that many would find ways to use these exact words when describing themselves during their interviews for the training program.

This company is probably quite aware of the candidate preconditioning caused by their lobby poster, and no doubt their interviewers are not taken in by candidates who repeat these words back to them. But what about your company? Even if you have not been profiled in the business press, your annual report can give clear signals about your culture to candidates who are willing to do their homework. One of the most telling sections for conveying your organization's culture is the president's message to stockholders. It describes current priorities and often reflects them against long-held values and beliefs.

Candidates are bombarded with advice about how to get interviewers to do most of the talking so they will reveal a great deal about their company. Tom Jackson's Guerrilla Tactic #69, how to get the employer to describe what he is looking for in the beginning of the interview, was cited in Chapter 3. Jackson expands on this point: "Most recruiters will give you a description of what they are looking for. Pay attention, take mental notes. For the balance of the interview, feed back to the recruiter the things he has said he is looking for."

As an interviewer, you can match the candidate's preparation by:

1. Knowing your own company culture and its implications for hiring, and

2. Knowing how to interview and get behind the extensive preparation of today's candidates.

Any business or organization big enough to hire can benefit

from a look at its own culture and the techniques available for finding the right candidates who will fit in successfully. In fact, business success through the '80s and into the '90s will *demand* this way of interviewing and hiring others. Chapter 7 will show you how to apply these concepts to the hiring process.

Is corporate culture worth all this fuss? I think so.

In the late 1970s, two major U.S. corporations brought new CEOs into their cultures from other companies. One adapted successfully, and the company prospered. The other CEO failed, and the company suffered enormously. Perhaps you can guess who they were: Lee Iacocca at Chrysler and Archie McCardell at International Harvester.

A 1985 *Time* magazine cover story on Iacocca discussed the growing interest in him as a U.S. presidential candidate. Concerns about his success in that job really hang on one question: fit between job culture and candidate qualities. *Time* noted that

> Iacocca likes getting his way in the world quickly and unambiguously. He is a bossy boss. Heads of corporations can fold whole departments, hire anybody they choose and, in Iacocca's phrase, "shuck the losers." Presidents, on the other hand, are hemmed in, constrained by the Executive bureaucracy, checked and balanced by Congress. In the give and take of governing, Iacocca's virtues—frankness, boldness—might not serve him so well.*

SUMMARY

Culture and candidate must fit. The techniques and skills offered in this book will provide readers with a method for interviewing candidates that will help insure the best possible fit. When considering the critical match-up of candidates to culture, you can apply a basic principle to all interviewing: The hiring process really boils down to fitting people against jobs. To fit people against jobs in a way

---

*Time, April 1, 1985.

that considers a candidate's important fit with your culture, you need to predetermine the *behaviors* required to succeed on the job. Culture is determined by the *how* of each job, and most job descriptions only tell the *what*: what is required, what is paid, what the benefits are, what the reporting function is, or what skills are required. Today's candidates have been coached in ways to identify and use corporate culture in their interviews. Today's interviewers must be prepared to do the same.

7

The Candidate/Job Profile

Jobs don't really exist by themselves, they are merely concepts. They become real when you describe them in terms of a person in a specific situation.

Anonymous

T he cultural description of an organization should be reflected in a candidate/job profile and used as a context for considering candidates during the interview process. This begins with awareness of the qualities required for the position (*how* the person will do the job) as well as the duties and responsibilities (*what* the person must do). Consider this brief description for the position of Treasury Manager with a major manufactured goods importer.

Treasury Manager

Will manage the company's treasury function, including an investment portfolio representing several hundred million dollars. Must develop and implement short- and long-term funding strategies. Will supervise the Cash Management Manager and staff. Reports to Corporate Finance Manager and works closely with Senior Vice President Finance and Administration. The ideal candidate will be a CPA or have an MBA in Finance and have 10–15 years in treasury-related positions in leading industrial firms or major financial institutions. Some experience in international financial matters and knowledge of foreign banks is highly desirable.

While providing clear information about *what* the person must do in this job, and the education and experience required, there is little in this description that says *how* the job must be done. Consider how a manager's focus on desired qualities in the candidate will shift by *adding* the following to this description:

Organizational Culture

Multiculture environment where harmonious working relations are important. People are involved in goal-setting through mutual give and take. Communications take place in an informal way, through natural influence groups. Commitment to excellence a shared value.

This culture statement adds significant implications to the job description. A person qualified for this position would have not only the education and experience (Resume Factor) described in the first part of the description, but important *qualities* in the three Performance Factor areas that might include:

Intellectual
Articulate
Strategic thinker

Interpersonal
Tactful
Patient

Motivational
Ambitious
Wants financial career

Most people have not been trained to view positions in this way. The value of this perspective is that it establishes a framework for behavioral interviewing that permits the interviewer to look for qualities that will be essential to success on the job. But it goes further. By reflecting the culture of the entire organization (or division or department) it also helps insure that the person will fit not only with the job, but with the organization. The potential for advancement and retention of the employee is thus enhanced.

WHERE THE JOB DESCRIPTION LEAVES OFF

A major handicap managers face when they interview is that they have so little help in defining what they should be looking for to fit candidates into their culture. If they use a conventional job description, they are up against the limitation that it describes a job only in terms of duties and responsibilities.

Job descriptions are used to distinguish one job or job family from another. They describe *what* must be done on the job, not *how* it must be done. They don't describe behavioral factors required for success on the job. Instead, they emphasize rational, measurable factors and are typically used for "objective" decisions such as salary, office size, furniture, etc. Their usefulness in conducting an interview is very limited.

Many organizations will require that a job requisition be completed and approved before candidate sourcing and interviewing begins. Requisitions aren't much help either. These micro-summaries of job descriptions tend to describe job duties in the briefest of terms. For example, here is an exact quote from a requisition used by one organization: "Prepare, release and maintain engineering standards, procedures and guidelines to manage, control and develop software programs." This description of a Senior Engineer gives no clues as to what behavioral traits will contribute to success on the job.

Because of these shortcomings of traditional job descriptions, it is understandable why interviewers often take the candidate's resume as the only useful guide they've got to conduct the interview. This chapter provides an alternative to these frustrating conditions. It's called a candidate/job profile.

This profile recognizes the influence of an organization's culture and the specific job situation on the qualities to be sought in each interview. This behavioral-based job description helps managers get behind the candidate's resume and interview in a way that determines a candidate's behavioral fit with your job and organizational culture.

The candidate/job profile starts where traditional job descriptions end, which is with a list of duties and responsibilities. It considers the culture and situation of the job in a way that produces a list of candidate behavioral specifications—in other words, *how* the job must be done.

To develop a useful statement about your organizational culture, you should consider culture and the job situation separately. However, in reality, they are tightly integrated.

DEFINING CORPORATE CULTURE

As defined in the previous chapter, corporate culture has two major components: shared values and common beliefs.

Shared values represent important attitudes people should have to perform their job successfully. "Customer service" is a shared value at IBM; "product quality" is becoming one at Ford. At Apple Computer, "Third Wave" thinking—or a sense of mission about their work—is a shared value among employees.

Common beliefs describe employee attitudes about how things are done in their company. Citibank assumes people will take chances. Goldman Sachs expects people to put in long hours. Successful people at Apple have a pattern of looking for solutions, not presenting problems. The *100 Best Companies* book points out that Intel is "a place where 'constructive confrontation' takes place, where arguing and fighting are encouraged...."

A cultural anthropologist could define a list of shared values and common beliefs for your organization. Without the time or access to such advice, try a few exercises on your own or with a group of peers to produce descriptive statements of your organization and its work style.

One way to do this is to list the major pluses and minuses for working at your organization. Many qualities will stand out as an immediate plus (sophisticated clients) or an immediate minus (variability in industry direction). You may see, however, that some qualities show up on both lists. A plus quality of "rapidly changing" also suggests a negative of "uncertainty." If you are "lean and fast-paced," you might face "long hours and the risk of burnout."

Once you have this list, consider the kind of people who are most likely to fit in. Develop a list of descriptive words and use them to complete this statement: "Successful people here tend to be ...." Use words such as the following, if appropriate: bright, articulate, street smart, creative, analytical, buttoned-up, intuitive. Other possibilities: aggressive, competitive, conservative, conforming, diligent, entrepreneurial, flexible, hard-working, personable, systems-oriented, energetic.

As you list these qualities, you will find your thinking begins to focus less on the corporate level and more on your department and specific job situation.

DEFINING THE JOB SITUATION

An analysis of the job situation adds a dimension of immediacy and local impact to the overall influence of corporate culture. The situation surrounding your open job may now be heavily influenced by external factors. For example, the marketplace in which you compete may be changing.

In the personal computer market, the shift is from being technology-driven to being consumer-driven. This can affect the hiring of product development engineers, who may now need added skills to relate to consumers as well as traditional engineering skills.

Insurance sales people may historically have succeeded with personality traits of aggressiveness and persistence. Today's sophisticated market will now respond to a more consultative type of selling that requires winning customer trust and being viewed as a problem-solver.

Traditional functions within an organization may require new skills for survival in a more competitive world. If the marketing function must now account for cash tied up in finished goods inventory, then a more hard-nosed, bottom-line financial orientation may become necessary for individual success in the marketing department.

A job that is open today may present very different challenges than it would a year from now. Here are two different situations facing a new department manager. In situation A, the department has poor operating effectiveness, low morale, and high turnover. The new manager must quickly turn this situation around. He or she should have the qualities of a seasoned, tough, self-confident, and decisive manager.

In situation B (the same job a year from now), the department is well-run and performing strongly. The challenge is to sustain the momentum. The new manager should have wisdom and maturity and should not be motivated by a desire to make a quick mark for himself. The person who is successful in situation A may not be the person for situation B.

These examples underscore the need to continually evaluate the situational influences on jobs in your organization.

Considerations that can help managers assess the situational aspects of a job can be grouped under the following headings: marketplace influence, position history, current priorities, future changes, and the working team.

Marketplace Influence

Look at changes in the marketplace that require the job to be handled differently than it has been. If the market is changing so rapidly that it's not clear where it is going to shake out, it is important to recognize the need for someone who can deal with change, handle stress, and be resourceful.

Commercial loan officers in large money market banks now find they are competing for business with investment bankers. In addition to traditional skills like customer credit worthiness analysis and transaction banking, new skills are required, including consultative selling and relationship banking.

Position History

It is important to know why the job is open. If it is to replace someone who left, then the basis for the departure may carry implications about the next successful candidate. If the person was promoted out of the job, presumably he or she had qualities that led to career growth within the company, and a replacement should have some of those same qualities.

If the previous incumbent was fired or transferred out of the job, the reasons for that person's failure should be reviewed. Did the person lack financial skills? Sales ability? Adaptability to desktop computers? Use these checkpoints to avoid hiring a new person who also lacks those qualities. But don't hire only to correct a deficiency revealed by the last person to hold this job. Make sure the candidate has other strengths as well. Ideally, you will constantly upgrade as you hire replacements.

If this is a new position created by reorganization or expansion, the person selected must not only define the job but win acceptance for it as well. The person selected must have enough drive to make the job happen but must also possess the people skills to gain organizational acceptance for the new position.

Current Priorities

The previous description of situation A suggests a number of current priorities that call for special skills to stem turnover, improve morale, and upgrade operating results.

On a less dramatic scale, the job may have special needs that currently require attention and make last year's job description somewhat obsolete. For example, it may now be necessary to start up a new reporting procedure in this job, or use a computer terminal to access information directly, or start making sales calls on distributors as well as retailers. Each of these current priorities suggests qualities you should now be looking for when you interview candidates.

Future Changes

Hiring decisions are difficult to reverse. Therefore, it's wise to anticipate future changes in the job so the person you hire today will not become only a marginal fit with what's required six months or a year from now.

A company may project that its sales will soon plateau after several years of rapid growth. In this new situation, the financial emphasis will shift from growth to cost avoidance and control. Criteria for managers newly hired in the financial function should incorporate skills needed in this predictable new environment, not just the current job situation.

If a company plans to reduce production staff and rely more on subcontractors, then managers they hire today may soon need to demonstrate purchasing and negotiating skills which are not yet required on the job.

Other predictable changes may be overlooked in the pressure of trying to fill the current opening. The scope of this job may expand (or contract) when the new fiscal year commences.

For example, the recruiting function within personnel may soon be expected to retain responsibility for college relations (contact with the school placement offices) and train line managers to take over and handle college recruiting (on-campus interviews) directly. Planning and administrative skills may soon be more important in this job than willingness to travel and do lots of interviewing.

In a final consideration, the job may be one where new hires will begin to get exposure and training within the company. Skills in training others may become important for the first time.

Don't hire a new person for a job as it is defined today if you know of predictable future changes that will influence what will be needed for success in that job tomorrow.

The Working Team

Important working relationships with the supervisor, co-workers, and subordinates also must be considered if you want to hire effectively.

When a job becomes vacant, ask others who will work with the new person what *they* want from the position. Your questions along this line can include, "What do you depend on the person in this job for?" "How do you count on the person in that job to help you do your job?" You can use their answers to help define the kind of person you want.

If the job largely involves dealing with those outside the company—customers, clients, distributors, and vendors—visualize the kind of person who will work most effectively with them on your behalf. Describe that ideal person in behavioral terms—forceful, quick-witted, patient, accommodating, etc. Include these words in your candidate/job profile.

WHAT A PROFILE SHOULD CONTAIN

A completed candidate/job profile identifies on a single page the job duties, the organizational culture, and the behavioral factors sought in a candidate.

What follows is an example of one for a food and beverage analyst in a major hotel.

HOTEL

POSITION—Food and Beverage Analyst

DUTIES

Implement food and beverage control system; prepare sales and cost analysis of menus and beverages; solve operational problems within F&B Dept. Must work effectively with all Department Heads and Personnel.

CULTURE

Busy, demanding workplace and job requirements. Office in high-traffic area next to goods receiving. Frequent interruptions, including periodic work as restaurant manager. Storeroom audits and current major hotel refurbishing program will require someone willing to "get their hands dirty" while doing this job.

FACTORS

Resume

- Hotel school; kitchen experience a plus
- Knowledge of accounting procedures
- Understanding of computers

Intellectual

- Analytical, precise
- Balance of fact and feeling in decision making
- Good memory

Interpersonal

- Personable
- Methodical
- Persistent, even stubborn

Motivational

- Interest in hotel's interest and guest satisfaction
- Motivation to self-teach
- Wants a fast pace and respect of others

This hotel example reflects the enormous importance of the local situation, and does not reflect a broader statement such as shared values and common beliefs held corporatewide by this international hotel.

Both the statement about duties and the one about culture set up the need for specific qualities under the Resume Factor and the three Performance Factors.

In terms of duties, to solve operational problems within the food and beverage department, the candidate needs to be "persistent, even stubborn," an interpersonal trait. Cost analysis of menus and beverages requires someone who is "methodical"—also an interpersonal trait.

Relative to the culture in this hotel situation, the F&B analyst may face periodic work as a restaurant manager. Therefore, previous kitchen experience is listed as a desirable plus under the Resume Factor. Storeroom audits are more easily handled if the candidate has a good memory—an intellectual quality. The pace of the job also calls for a certain kind of motivation.

The six candidate/job profiles at the end of this chapter reflect a variety of organizations—from high-technology companies to banks and consulting firms.

Notice in each whether the individual Performance Factors listed are set up by the duties of the job or by the culture of the organization. A common interpersonal factor sought in several of the profiles that follow is self-confidence. The trigger statement for this quality is listed in the cultural description of the computer company and the aerospace firm:

Computer Company—Employee's ability and confidence level on the job are tested frequently.

Aerospace—Requires a willingness to correct problems or reward performance on the spot.

The need to be practical or pragmatic—an intellectual factor— is set up by the duties in the bank and consulting firm profiles:

Bank—Requires ... a practical decision-making style.

Engineering Consulting Firm—Represent clients at regulatory meetings (where pragmatism is necessary).

SUMMARY

Job descriptions take on meaning when the organizational culture and specific job situation are considered. Both elements set up behavioral factors with which to describe a suitable candidate. The candidate/job profile prepares interviewers for moving from the *what* to the *how* in interviewing candidates.

COMPUTER COMPANY

POSITION—Manager, Creative Services

DUTIES

Manage Creative Services Group for entire company. Must provide leading-edge work on time and on budget and assure that all creative work is consistent with plans from the marketing groups.

CULTURE

A fast-paced environment where people are expected to make quick decisions, sometimes without a lot of data. Employee's ability and confidence level on the job are tested frequently. A lack of formal procedures requires individual flexibility. Results are achieved by building relationships and cooperation, not with formal titles or demands made on others.

FACTORS

Resume

- 10 years prior design experience
- Has managed "great" creative people
- B.A. in graphic design

Intellectual

- Creative
- Quick decision maker
- Articulate

Interpersonal

- Enthusiastic
- Self-confident
- Responsive

Motivational

- Drive
- Project-work energy
- Multi-interests in design and merchandising

AEROSPACE COMPANY

POSITION—Team Leader, Structure Research

DUTIES

Must provide innovative and creative solutions to complex structure mechanics problems. Will originate research programs; develop and apply new structural concepts; coordinate activities and provide technical leadership of a team. Will also establish resource requirements and help select people.

CULTURE

A rapidly growing organization currently lacking formal structure and procedures. Advanced R&D done in an environment where consensus-building is important among a highly committed engineering staff. Requires a willingness to correct problems or reward performance on the spot. Support for individual development is a company value.

FACTORS

Resume

– Ph.D. plus 10 years experience (or M.S. plus 15)
– Prefer 2-3 years in aerospace industry
– Government, university, or private research experience

Intellectual

– Bright
– Creative
– Articulate (written and oral)

Interpersonal

– Self-confident
– Works well with others
– Self-disciplined

Motivational

– Enjoys problem solving
– Has tireless energy
– Responds to freedom from controlled supervision

COMMERCIAL BANK

POSITION—Capital Markets, Financial Trader

DUTIES

Trade bonds, currencies, and money market instruments to maintain daily reserves for the bank. Requires strong skills in computer-based financial analysis and a practical decision making style to maximize trading results.

CULTURE

Environment is exciting, hectic, fast-paced and pressured, where creativity and innovation are encouraged. "Sink or swim" climate, not long-term training program, is used to sort people out.

FACTORS

Resume

- Broad business perspective
- MBA with strong finance background
- Knowledge of computers

Intellectual

- Smart
- Analytical
- Pragmatic
- Innovative
- Articulate
- Decisive

Interpersonal

- Self-confident
- Outgoing, personable
- Can handle stress
- Persuasive
- Aggressive

Motivational

- Likes numbers, transactions, strategies (poker, etc.)
- Seeks a challenge; high risk/reward ratio
- High energy

ENGINEERING CONSULTING FIRM

POSITION—Project Manager

DUTIES

Review and set staff assignments within group; day-to-day coordination of assigned projects; direct interface with client's project director; represent project for client at regulatory meetings; first-line review of responsibility for project budget; approval of monthly billing statements; periodic in-field review of project quality and adherence to project plan; detailed review and approval of all project documents; emphasis on technical accuracy and consistency.

CULTURE

Professional, fast-paced work environment requiring competent project management, often interdisciplinary in scope. Will deal with sophisticated, demanding clients, often in high-stress problem areas that require quick and confident response.

FACTORS

Resume

- Registered geologist with 7–10 years experience
- Prior consulting experience in hydrogeology
- B.S. degree required; M.S. desirable

Intellectual

- Practical
- Articulate (written and oral)
- Analytical, trouble shooter

Interpersonal

- Mature, responsible
- Self-confident, can handle stress
- Persuasive, especially with regulatory people

Motivational

- Seeks project diversity
- Financial rewards important
- Hard-working, likes people

UNIVERSITY

POSITION—Purchasing Manager

DUTIES

Responsible for planning, organizing, directing, and controlling all aspects of the university's Purchasing Department. Supervises a staff of 34 full-time employees and processes more than $100 million in procurement transactions annually. Has primary responsibility for interpreting, restating, redefining, and proposing improvements in existing policy and for proposing new policies for purchasing.

CULTURE

Purchasing Department has a strong commitment to excellence and views the needs of its clients as critical to its success. Goals are prioritized after careful assessment, and leaders involve others in the implementation of these goals. Information about decisions and events is openly communicated. Employees are encouraged to further their own professional growth and development.

FACTORS

Resume

- General knowledge of college and university supply process
- Working knowledge of traditional, nontraditional and state-of-the-art purchasing methods
- Knows application of EDP systems to the supply process
- Working knowledge of university system purchasing policies and procedures
- Experience administering complex financial processes and budgets

Intellectual

- Analytical and decisive
- Good written and oral communication skills
- Strong problem-solving skills

Interpersonal
- Self-confident, able to resist pressure
- Authoritative
- Able to motivate others and work collaboratively

Motivational
- Results-oriented
- High energy level

SEMICONDUCTOR COMPANY

POSITION—Director of Technology

DUTIES

Reports to President. Directs all R&D activities and supports manufacturing as the company starts full-scale production of a rapid thermal processing system. Will staff and manage the R&D function.

CULTURE

Start-up company with equity opportunity. Currently moving from development to manufacturing stage. Director will manage a staff of scientists and engineers, many with advanced degrees. Leanly staffed, high-growth environment calls for results-oriented work style and teamwork.

FACTORS

Resume

- Advanced degree, prefer Ph.D.
- Academic focus on solid state physics
- Experience in semiconductor processing

Intellectual

- Analytical
- Problem solver
- Creative

Interpersonal

- Dependable
- Competitive
- Team player

Motivational

- Willing to work long hours as needed
- High project-related energy
- Motivated by a challenge

8

Setting a Mood for the Interview

*Relaxation is as important as any of the other techniques
suggested in this book. But it almost needs to be treated
with an admonition because the more one tries to achieve
it, the further he tends to move in the opposite direction.**

H. Anthony Medley
Sweaty Palms: The Neglected Art of Being Interviewed

O ne of the aspects of the interview that is easiest for you to
control is the mood or climate in which you conduct it. You
need a strategy to do this effectively.

Revealing interviews occur when the candidate is relaxed. For
this reason, "stress interviews" are not recommended in this book.
There is a time during behavioral interviewing when it is appropriate
to ask questions that produce some stress. These techniques are
covered in Chapter 15. In general, however, selection interviews are
more productive when the mood of the interview is nonthreatening
and accepting.

If you can set the proper climate for this, the people you inter-

---

*H. Anthony Medley, *Sweaty Palms: The Neglected Art of Being Interviewed* (Berkeley, CA: Ten Speed
Press, 1984).

view will probably end up telling you a great deal about themselves—perhaps even more than they intended to say.

This supports the outcome you want from the interview: to learn all you possibly can about candidates so you can predict on-the-job behavior.

The techniques you use to do this are similar to those you would use with a new customer, client, or co-worker you meet for the first time in your office.

In those situations you want the customer, client, or co-worker to tell you about themselves—the things that are important to them, the things they respond to, what they're interested in, what they want. Keep that same picture in mind when you prepare to meet a new candidate for the job.

There are a number of things you can do to establish a feeling of comfort and relaxation in an interview. When these things are not done, a candidate can feel uncomfortable and under stress. This limits what you will learn.

The following suggestions will help you set the right mood or climate.

GO OUT TO GREET THE PERSON

If you walk out of your office to escort the candidate back to your office for the interview, you signal an unspoken concern and interest. When you greet the person in this way, the candidate is less likely to feel as though he or she is being summoned to your office for a judgment-type interview.

USE SMALL TALK WISELY

Small talk that's relevant to the person being interviewed can contribute to a relaxed interview climate.

"I notice you grew up in the Midwest—so did I," is relevant

small talk. "How about those Giants?" is not necessarily relevant to the person—the candidate may not be interested in baseball (or may think you mean the Giants football team) and may feel uncomfortable about being unable to respond. Use of small talk should be limited. Extended use of irrelevant small talk begins to build tension and reinforces the idea that the interviewer is in command and will discuss any topic he or she chooses—regardless of its relevance to the candidate or the position. This does not relax the candidate.

PUT OUT A WELCOME MAT

The setting in your office should be welcoming and informal. No matter what size your office, you should avoid sitting behind your desk during the interview. Find two comfortable chairs and sit opposite but near the candidate. If your office is small, try to find an unused office or meeting room that will provide a more relaxed setting.

Interviewers who remain behind their desks establish a distance between themselves and the candidate that can suggest a courtroom atmosphere. An interview should not be a trial. By sitting closer to the candidate, the interviewer helps establish a climate in which the candidate feels more like an equal and is thus more likely to be responsive and at ease.

If you are comfortable working in your shirtsleeves, you might even hang up your jacket and offer to do the same for the candidate.

Treat the person being interviewed like a guest in your home, not like a salesperson or unwelcome visitor.

AVOID INTERRUPTIONS

You should avoid being interrupted when you interview. Co-workers would not bother you if you were with a major client or customer: don't let them interrupt you during an interview. If your office is a partitioned space—a common setup in some industries—

or if you share it with a co-worker, then find a suitable unused space where you can have privacy.

Do not take telephone calls while interviewing. For many interviewers, this is more a habit than a necessity. If the one key call you must take from your major customer is likely to occur during the interview, explain and apologize for this before the interview begins. But, as a general principle, have your calls held. If there is no one to pick up your phone while you interview, then unplug it.

These techniques are very important, because interruptions give the candidate the idea that this interview is a low priority with you. This can make the candidate tense and uncomfortable. Such interruptions also sacrifice a natural advantage you have as an interviewer—they give the candidate *time to think* about the interview up to that point. They break the flow of the interview and your concentration. The candidate uses these interruptions to go back over what has been said, and his or her perception of your reaction. You may lose your advantage because the candidate will begin to correct or compensate for certain disclosures when the interview resumes.

USE COMPLIMENTS

Acknowledge achievements mentioned by candidates. If they are proudly telling you about something they have done, compliment them on the accomplishment.

"You seem very proud that your system was used by others." Your failure to comment on achievements in this way can make candidates feel they are not doing well in the interview. This can result in tension—just the opposite of what you want.

PLAY DOWN BAD NEWS

Anything revealed by a candidate that is not positive can be very threatening to the climate in the interview. Your success to date could be jeopardized at any point.

To handle these revelations ("I haven't had a raise in two years") you need to play down the importance of this while getting the person to elaborate further.

Here's one way: "Well, in this economy I guess lots of people are finding it more difficult to get a raise. What's been your situation for the last two years?"

This response from you will keep the interview open and minimize hiding of the "bad news." It should lead to an explanation of the "no salary increase," which is something you really want to know about.

ENCOURAGE ELABORATION

When you accept what you hear without condemning or condoning it, you are using a technique called "acceptance."

This approach involves phrases like "I see" or "That's interesting" or "Tell me more." These statements are lubricants to conversation and encourage the candidate to keep talking. They are especially useful for drawing out someone who tends to give you short answers.

Nonjudgmental responses from you help sustain a relaxed climate and give a conversational tone to the interview.

AVOID PROVOCATION

I once interviewed a woman for a professional position who practically opened the interview with this statement: "As far as I am concerned, you can divide the whole world into the lazy, gutless or the smart, hardworking."

My first reaction was to pounce on her statement and tell her I felt it was ridiculous to divide the whole world into such camps. I resisted this temptation and allowed her to demonstrate her unique attitude throughout the interview. This gave me ample evidence that she had, in fact, revealed an unacceptable attitude in the first few minutes of the interview.

Because I avoided a confrontation, I acquired evidence of numerous other attitudes and beliefs from her that I used later to defeat her candidacy for the job. If I had argued back immediately, I would probably have missed these other revelations. The evidence was necessary to overcome the acceptance of others who had also interviewed her that day and wanted to hire her because she was "tough" and "no pushover."

Sometimes, you may hear something from a candidate that is a factual (as opposed to an attitudinal) disqualifier. In this case, you should clear it up immediately.

A candidate you are interviewing may have a two-year gap in his chronological resume. If you say, "I see your last job was from 1979 to 1985—where have you been since then?" and the candidate responds, "Attica Prison" or "The New York Methadone Treatment Center for Severe Drug Addiction," you have to deal with this on the spot. You can't just say, "Well, tell me about your hobbies and leisure time interests," or "What was it about Attica Prison that you particularly liked?"

SUMMARY

The quality and richness of the interview you conduct is significantly influenced by the climate you set for it in your office.

You can't control the weather when you plan a picnic—you just hope for a sunny day. When you interview a candidate for a job, you *can* control the climate. Have a strategy to keep it open and relaxed.

9

The Interview Model

Most of the time, if you give people a half-way decent opening question, they end up telling you fairly interesting things.*

Ted Koppel
Host, ABC-TV's "Nightline"

Once you have used the techniques suggested in Chapter 8 to establish the climate and mood for the interview, you will want to signal the candidate that the actual interview is about to begin. Be clear with the applicant that the small talk is over.

"Well, Harry, now it's time for me to learn something about you and your background. During our interview, I'm going to let you do most of the talking. Then, toward the end of the interview, I'll give you a chance to ask me some questions about our company and the position that's open. We'll have about an hour together, so let's get started."

This opening statement gives the candidate an idea about how you expect the interview to flow and when it will be the proper time

---

*Quoted by Nancy Collins in "The Smartest Man on TV," *New York Magazine,* Aug. 13, 1984.

for him or her to ask questions. By using such a statement, you establish control of the interview process at the outset.

You are now ready to apply a specific model and conduct an effective interview.

ELEMENTS

The recommended interview model for drawing out many examples of candidate behavior starts with a very expansive question called a *Topic Opener* (see Chapter 16). This question is followed with more specific questions that flow naturally from the candidate's responses to the Topic Opener. These later questions allow candidates to develop specific aspects of their broad answers.

This model can be visualized as a funnel or a pie piece. As you move down a funnel or pie piece, you go from the widest part to the narrowest. In an interview, this means that you move from the *Topic Opener*, through *Self-Appraisal Questions* (Chapter 17) and finally to *Situation-Based Questions* (Chapter 18). Although each of these question types is developed fully in these later chapters, let's briefly consider them here as they relate to the model.

The Topic Opener

Topic-Opener questions are concerned with a broad topic or time period in the candidate's education and experience. These questions allow the candidate to construct an answer and select information that will give you plenty of information on which to base follow-up questions. It's important to keep this question broad. When we narrow the Topic Opener it loses its impact and can telegraph an answer. "Tell me about your leadership activities in college" is too narrow and telegraphs a possible priority. It is also important not to make the Topic Opener too broad: "Tell me about your life" is too unfocused. "Tell me about your college years" is a good Topic Opener.

Self-Appraisal Questions

Self-Appraisal questions are used to follow up on the information gathered during the candidate's responses to Topic Opener questions. These questions ask the candidate to explain a fact or accomplishment, and thus provide insights that move the interview from a focus on the Resume Factor to inferences about the candidate's three Performance Factors. Answers to Self-Appraisal questions help the interviewer begin to generate behavioral premises about the candidate. These insights help develop a composite picture of the candidate by the end of the interview.

Situation-Based Questions

Situation-Based questions are the most specific. They occur near the narrow end of the funnel or the pie piece. These questions allow you to learn what candidates have done or might do in specific situations (*Problem Situation*); how they view themselves relative to certain tasks, circumstances or choices (*Comparison* and *Continuum*); and what predictions they have for their performance if they are hired (*Future Assessment*).

The Wrap-Up Question

The wrap-up question, like the opening statement, signals the candidate that a major shift in the flow of the interview is occurring. It too is an essential tool in your control of the interview. It can be used to wrap up each topic area as well as the overall interview.

After you have covered a variety of topics to your satisfaction, you are ready to conclude the evaluative phase of the interview. You need a way to wrap up your questioning and give the candidate time to ask questions.

When you reach this point in the interview, say to the candidate, "I appreciate your thoughtful answers to my questions. Now it's your turn. Is there anything else you would like to tell me about yourself?" Or you may ask, "Is there anything we have not covered that you feel I should know about you?"

Not only does this let the candidate know you have reached the end of your questioning, it also gives the candidate a final chance to add something else that's important. Despite all you have covered, there still may be some major accomplishment, event, or concern the candidate would like to mention. The wrap-up question allows that to happen.

The model looks like this:

TOPIC-OPENER QUESTION
SELF-APPRAISAL QUESTIONS
SITUATION-BASED QUESTIONS
PROBLEM SITUATION
CONTINUUM
COMPARISON
FUTURE ASSESSMENT
WRAP-UP QUESTION

This basic model can be applied to six or more major topics or time periods. Envision a completed interview as looking like a pie, sliced into six pieces.

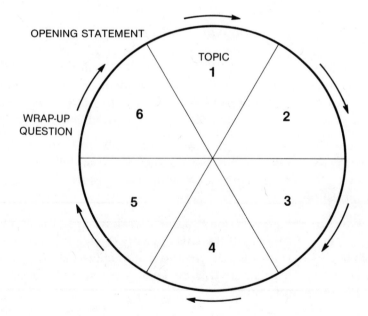

TOPICS GUIDE THE INTERVIEW

The topics you can explore with this model encompass what's on any resume. More importantly, this approach insures that you will *get behind the resume*. You will be in control because the interview will focus on *your* topics, not the candidate's resume.

During my career, I have glanced at probably more than 20,000 resumes and read several thousand of them carefully. Based on this experience, and what I've read in books that advise job seekers about resume writing, the following list covers what's on any resume:

Job objective
Experience
      Current job
      Previous job(s)
Accomplishments
Education
      Graduate school
      College
      Other
Service
      Military, Peace Corps
Other
      Professional associations
      Published works
      Hobbies and leisure interests
      Travel

Many managers feel they can't interview without referring to a resume. They tend to use the resume as a prop, asking questions that merely verify the information that is already stated or questions that add little to their understanding of how well the candidate might perform on the job. "I see you worked at Xerox. I know some people there—who did you work with?" This seems like a natural and easy way to conduct an interview. Unfortunately, it allows the candidate to strongly influence what is covered in the interview because it is based on what he or she presented to you on the resume.

The model described in this chapter allows you to conduct an interview that will yield the kind of information you need to assess a candidate's potential fit with a job. Here are six topics to be explored in an interview, using the recommended interviewing model:

Current job
Prior job(s)
Accomplishments
Career goals
Education
Other

Advantages

There are six advantages to using this list of topics with the interview model.

▶ *It's simple.* The model employs three major questions which you use with each of six topics. You follow the model with each topic area. If your interview is not long enough to cover all the topics, then plan in advance that another interviewer will cover the rest. If you remember that the model is shaped like a funnel or pie piece, the simple diagram on page 91 will help you visualize how the model works.

▶ *It's effective.* This list of topics covers many aspects of the candidate's life and career, thus permitting a broad array of job-related premises to surface during the interview. When the interview model is used to explore each of these topics, a great deal of information is generated from which the interviewer can draw behavioral inferences. Evidence of certain skills and behaviors will be repeated as the candidate describes many different accomplishments and time periods. At the end of the interview, you will have repeated confirmation of premises that will enable to you make an objective and substantiated decision.

▶ *It's flexible.* You can vary the topics. For someone right out of school with little or no work experience and few job-related accomplishments you can drop topic areas such as current job, prior jobs(s), and accomplishments and add high school education,

Topics:

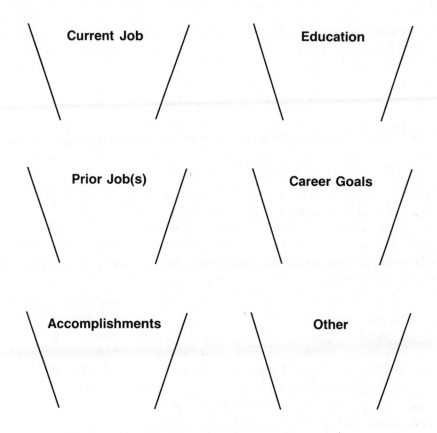

Current Job

Education

Prior Job(s)

Career Goals

Accomplishments

Other

part-time jobs, and leisure time interests. For someone reentering the work force, these are some appropriate topics:

Career goals
Volunteer experience
Part-time work
Previous work experience
Leisure time activities

▶ *It provides variety.* You can alter the choice, number, and order of the topics for any interview. You can start with any topic you have selected, then move up or down your list as appropriate. When interviewing an experienced candidate, it can liven the interview if you start back in time and move forward chronologically. Because this is the opposite sequence of most resumes, it may catch the glib candidate off guard. An advantage to this reverse order is that you also can see what choices the candidate made, hear about the roads not taken, and begin to infer patterns in the candidate's behavior that may help you when it's time to make your decision.

▶ *It keeps you in control.* Your control comes from several factors. You can start the interview with any appropriate topic. You decide when to move from one topic to another. You always know where you are going in an interview because you know what topic comes next. If a topic is yielding a rich set of behavioral inferences, you can stay with it longer. If a topic is not very productive, you can move to the next one. The balance of control is determined by you, not by the candidate's highly polished resume.

▶ *Topics are thoroughly covered.* The Topic-Opener question insures that each major area is opened up fully in the interview. When you open the topic of education by saying to a candidate, "Tell me about your years at Dartmouth," you avoid becoming overly specific too early in the interview. This broad entry is far preferable to a the following question: "I see you went to Dartmouth. Did you belong to a fraternity?" This makes the question of fraternity affiliation the first thing you talk about, possibly overshadowing some other pertinent information about college experience that the candidate would otherwise reveal. Give the candidate a chance to elaborate on his Dartmouth experience. Then you can begin to focus on particular accomplishments and facts using the other parts of the interview model. In this way, you cover the topic thoroughly.

THE INTERVIEW MODEL VS. THE Q&A APPROACH

Interviews conducted according to this model are just the opposite of a question-and-answer interrogation-style interview. Interviewers who use lots of specific probing questions may put the candidate on the defensive. This can lead to a series of short, prisoner-of-war type responses!

The question-and-answer approach can turn a relaxed and friendly interview into a fact-gathering mission. As the conversation narrows, the interviewer has to work harder and harder to keep the interview going. There is increasing stress on the interviewer to try to think of the next question to ask. The focus can easily shift from listening to the candidate's answers to concentrating on what the next question will be.

Many interviewers alleviate this stress by starting to talk about the organization: "Let me tell you a little about our company . . ." At this point, the interview is effectively over. The interviewer is no longer learning about the candidate, but is instead talking about the job, the organization, or himself.

The interview model described in this chapter not only keeps you in control but also has been described by one interviewer as "user friendly!"

USING THE MODEL WITH MORE THAN ONE INTERVIEWER

Applying the interview model to a series of topics during an interview works well for Team and Panel interviews as well as in the individual application described above.

Team Interviews

Team interviews, for the purposes of this discussion, are defined as interviews that involve two interviewers and one candidate. The advantages of this type of interview are the powerful insights it can deliver and its efficiency when the candidate's time in your offices is limited. The disadvantages arise when untrained interviewers create a stressful interview for the candidate and an unproductive experience for the employer.

To get the most from a team interview, decide in advance on a specific role for each member of the team. A useful model for this is to have one person conduct the first two-thirds of the interview without interruption. The other team member listens and takes notes until the last one-third of the interview, then comes in with questions.

Or, in another version, each team member could handle specific topics during the interview. For example, one interviewer can cover the candidate's current job and the second can cover earlier career and educational experiences. Or, one interviewer can cover technical knowledge and expertise and the second interviewer can cover management style, working relationships, and career goals.

Revealing insights can emerge from a team interview, especially when one of the above-described approaches is used. Because one interviewer listens while the other interviews, there is an opportunity for the second interviewer to follow up on inconsistencies or concerns that have come up in the first part of the interview. The second interviewer can be closely focused on these key issues within the context of the topic areas he or she will cover. When the interview is over, the team members can quickly compare observations and develop a complete evaluation of the interview and the candidate.

Team interviews, when the interviewers' roles are clearly defined, need not be stressful for the candidate. Problems arise when unskilled interviewers turn a team interview into a tennis match (taking turns asking questions which may be unconnected) or, worse, conduct a "good cop/bad cop" interrogation.

Stress in a team interview results from the interviewers' lack of planning and coordination. Interviewer One asks a question and the candidate's response invites a further probe or follow-up question. But Interviewer Two has been waiting for the chance to ask his or her favorite question, so, rather than listening and letting the first interviewer explore the candidate's answer, he or she jumps in with a question that disrupts the flow of information: "Could we go back to something you said earlier?" or "Could we move ahead now to talk about reasons for changing jobs at this time?"

Interviewer One has lost control of the questioning and the opportunity to follow up on the last answer. As this pattern is repeated, the candidate experiences stress and frustration.

By applying the interview model to a number of topics and defining roles for the interview, you should have success with team interviews. Here are three other pointers to make the most of this powerful technique.

▶ *Allow about 50 percent more time for this type of interview than for an individual interview.* If you normally take 45 minutes in a one-on-one interview, plan on at least one hour for a team interview.

▶ *Explain at the beginning of the interview the roles of the interviewers so the candidate knows what to expect.* "Bill and I are going to conduct what we call a team interview. I'll be interviewing you for most of the time, then Bill will be coming in during the last portion with some questions of his own." Or, "Bill will cover certain topics and I'll cover others."

▶ *Be sure the candidate knows at the outset that your interviewing partner is not just a scribe who listens and takes notes.* "We often conduct team interviews, and enjoy trading roles from one interview to the next. Today it's my turn to be the principal interviewer, but Bill will have a few questions of his own. And we'll both allow you time to ask us questions about the job and the company as we get near the end of the interview. Let me begin."

Panel Interviews

A panel interview involves three or more interviewers. The advantage of a panel interview for the employer is the opportunity it provides for a number of people to meet, see, and hear the candidate.

This type of interview is particularly prevalent in school districts, colleges, universities, and government agencies where interviews are conducted by search committees. In these and other settings, the panel interview may be so institutionalized that it will be difficult to win support for any change to improve its application.

However, by introducing the interview model and topic organization, the effectiveness of this method can be enhanced.

It is very important in this interview method to relax the candidate. Some school districts and colleges have been known to include as many as eight or nine interviewers on a panel. It is an overwhelming experience for most candidates to stand before such a tribunal. Anything interviewers can do to reduce the inquisitorial atmosphere will contribute to the success of the interview. Time should be allowed for panel members to introduce themselves, and the candidate should be given an opportunity to engage in informal conversation with the panel before the interview begins. Humor also helps break the tension.

Clear role definition for the interviewers is essential, for the reasons described in the section on Team Interviews. All panelists should agree to use the interview model. The panel then should decide which topics will be covered, who will cover them and who will be the lead interviewer. One panelist should conduct the major portion of the interview, applying the model to several key topics. The other panelists should listen, not interrupt, and wait until the appropriate time to apply the model and ask questions that follow up and help focus what they have heard.

By the time a candidate is interviewed by a panel, he or she should have had at least one in-depth individual interview with one or more members of the search committee. A panel interview should not be used for screening candidates. It should be a final step in gathering evaluations of prime candidates. Panel members who have not previously met the candidate should be briefed beforehand on initial premises developed from the individual interview(s). Then they can be alert to evidence of certain skills and traits others have identified that enhance the individual's candidacy.

Panel interviews have great value in certain settings and under certain circumstances. They should be conducted when they are the most appropriate method for evaluating a particular candidate, never just for the convenience of the employer.

Today's candidates are being coached in how to handle stress-producing interviews. Ted Pettus offers interviewees a counter-strategy for panel interviews:

In this situation you will find it very productive to ask a lot of questions. Direct each question to a particular person, not to the group. In his effort to answer you, he will be very careful not to embarrass himself in front of his fellow employees. He will often assume a defensive and cautious position, putting you in firm control.*

SUMMARY

The interview model, when applied to a series of topics, can insure the interviewer's control of the interview. Rather than being led by the candidate's resume, interviewers can select the areas *they* want to discuss and the order in which they want to discuss them. Whether applied to individual, team or panel interviews, interviewers will find this approach to be simple, flexible, effective and thorough—providing variety to the interview and generating the information needed to make critical hiring decisions.

*Theodore Pettus, *One on One: Win the Interview, Win the Job* (New York: Random House, 1979).

10

Questions and the Topic Opener

*Of course, the best interviewers give the least information,
leaving the responsibility more in your hands.**

Tom Jackson
Guerrilla Tactics in the Job Market

T he likelihood that you will gather during an interview the kind of
information that will help you make an informed hiring decision
depends upon the questioning techniques you use. Effective questioning techniques create effective interviews. This chapter and the
next two will discuss the three major types of questions that form the
heart of the interview model: Topic-Opener, Self-Appraisal, and Situation-Based. A discussion of these question types is best preceded by
a review of open-ended questions.

OPEN-ENDED QUESTIONS ENCOURAGE ELABORATION

Open-ended questions can't be answered with a simple yes or
no. You should use them comfortably and naturally in *every* situation
where you seek to gain information from others.

---

*Tom Jackson, *Guerrilla Tactics in the Job Market* (New York: Bantam Books, 1978).

Open-ended questions begin with words like *what, when, how,* and *why*. Television interviewer Barbara Walters says she feels her most important question is not her first, but her second—and it's usually "why": "Why did you. . .?" "Why didn't you. . .?" "Why can't you. . .?" While this approach is very successful in television interviews, employment interviewers are advised to take special precautions in their use of the word *why*. A why question often leads to an answer beginning with "Because." This may indicate that the question has challenged the interviewee's motives and placed him or her on the defensive.

When people answer a *why* question, it leaves them wondering if the interviewer thinks their answer is right or wrong. Open-ended questions beginning with "How," "What," or "When" don't have this effect and are less likely to lead to evasive or defensive answers. If the people you interview have a tendency to become guarded or defensive, check to see if you are using too many *why* questions.

While a group of lawyers was discussing this idea in our seminar, one provided a good example of the right and wrong way to start off a question: "Say your client calls and says his teenage son just punched another kid and has been charged with assault—and will you talk to his son? There is a wrong way and a right way to do this, and it revolves around the opening question to the teenager.

Wrong: 'Why did you hit the other person?'

Right: 'What happened?' "

The lawyer pointed out that the second question will yield more information and honesty because the person is less defensive, less likely to color his answer to please you. It may turn out that the teenager was provoked long before this incident. By using a question to encourage an open response, the lawyer gains more information on which to build his case.

Participants in our seminars who have considerable business or professional experience often feel they know all about open-ended questions. The way we help them self-check their style and monitor their own current practices is to ask them "Do you begin your questions with a verb: 'Did you. . .', 'Do you. . .', 'Will you. . .'?" Those who respond affirmatively are told they are using closed-end questions and thus setting themselves up for answers that are too short and not revealing.

To avoid this result, an interviewer can just put "how" or "what" or "when" in front of those same questions: "*How* do you delegate your work?" not "*Do* you delegate your work?"

CLUES ABOUT THE INTELLECTUAL FACTOR

Open-ended questions can also help reveal how a person makes decisions and deals with ambiguity. "What is your proudest accomplishment to date?" This question requires the candidate to decide among several choices and provide an answer. His or her decision-making will be reflected in this process as you consider how relevant, important, and recent the selected example is to your open job.

If the answer reflects something the candidate did long ago ("I made Eagle Scout when I was 14.") you can follow up with other open-ended questions to probe the relevance of that impressive accomplishment today ("How has that experience helped you in later years?").

The candidate is asked to handle ambiguity when you ask a question like "What are your goals?" Possible answers: "Raise a family and be happy" or "Become a department manager within three years." Neither answer is wrong, but it may be useful to know whether people seek clarification on your question *before* they answer. Do they assume they know what you mean, or do they seek to clear up any possible confusion by asking, "Would you like to know about my professional goals, or what I want out of life?"

Open-ended questions and the interview model give you a framework for applying the Topic Opener and other questioning techniques.

TOPIC-OPENER QUESTIONS

Topic Openers are open-ended questions that ask the candidate to cover a major topic or time period in his or her life. They typically begin with a phrase such as "Tell me about. . ." or "Tell me what you did. . .". This type of question is used to open each of the major topics recommended for the interview model.

Such questions give people room to roam in their minds before answering your question. You tend to get longer answers and better information.

Unskilled interviewers often use this technique improperly by saying, "Tell me about yourself." This is *too* broad and unfocused, creating stress or irritation in candidates. Instead, you should ask candidates to tell you about their current work, career aspirations, how they got started in this field, college years, or some other *specific* time period, event, achievement, or goal.

When you use a topic-opener question, you can use a little bridge of your own into whatever topic you want to cover: "It would be interesting for me to learn about the things you are doing now, so why don't you *tell me about your current work?*"

It's important for you to be comfortable with topic-opener questions, because using them is one of the best ways to get a reading on the Intellectual Factor in the interview—one of the toughest Performance Factors to read.

Asking a topic-opener question is like handing candidates a blank piece of paper. They have to conceptualize an answer, organize their thoughts, and respond as articulately as they can. In response to your question, and before your very eyes, they are demonstrating how they think on their feet.

One caution: When you use topic-opener questions, don't let the candidate hand the question back to you!

Interviewer: Tell me about your first supervisory experience.

Candidate: What do you want to know about it?

Interviewer: Whatever you think is important for me to know.

This insures that you won't end up telegraphing the answer you want—which may be what candidates want you to do before they respond.

Another mistake in using the topic-opener question occurs when interviewers open the question correctly but then link it into a series of qualifiers that needlessly limit its use. Don't say, "Tell me about your college years and how they prepared you to go into banking, particularly in the field of commercial loans."

A question that is qualified like that shuts off a natural discussion of many aspects of those college years. At this point in the interview, a major slice of the candidate's life has been introduced, which the candidate should be able to discuss from the standpoint of academic performance, extracurricular activities, and summer and part-time work experience.

Today, increasing numbers of college students "stop out" of school for a year or so. This can be a growth-and-development experience for them. A question that requires them to justify college years in terms of their preparation for a job in your company is needlessly restrictive. As noted earlier, the same limitation is placed when you ask immediately if the candidate belonged to a fraternity or sorority.

If the response you get to a topic-opener question is extremely short, ask for elaboration. For example, if you say "Tell me about your college years," the candidate may describe four years of his life in what seems like a nanosecond: "I went to Ohio State and majored in political science." "What else can you tell me about your college years?" is the right follow-up. An interview full of short answers to your topic opener questions may reveal someone who simply can't carry on a decent conversation.

On the other hand, an extremely rambling, long-winded answer may require you to interrupt. "Tell you about my college years? Well, I'll begin with the first day of school. The day we drove on campus it was really hot, about 90 degrees. We had to drive all over the place to find the freshman dorm. . .."

While frustrating, this answer to your first topic-opener question is also very revealing. It suggests that the person can't organize his or her thoughts and answer a question in a reasonable amount of time. The detail and length of the answer may also indicate some social insensitivity!

When I was a corporate employment manager, I heard this complaint about a newly hired employee: "We took Jack out to the customer for his first meeting, and the customer couldn't get a word in edgewise. Jack never stopped talking." At this point, someone else spoke up, "You know, I noticed that when I interviewed him. He never stopped talking!"

Open-ended and topic-opener questions can bring out this kind of behavior. If the candidate is hopelessly long-winded, you can step in and control the interview. It's important to recognize this behavior during the interview because, although it may be due to nervousness over the interview, it could correlate with what you'll see on the job if you hire the candidate.

SUMMARY

To conduct an effective interview, interviewers should use open-ended questions that encourage elaborative responses from candidates. "What," "when," and "how" questions bring out valuable information. "Why" questions should be used sparingly. They may put the candidate on the defensive and detract from the interview. Topic Openers are the most open of the open-ended questions you will use in the Interview Model. They require the candidate to select and organize information and then express it in a way that will give the interviewer insights into the intellectual and interpersonal Performance Factors. When using the topic-opener question, do not allow the candidate to hand it back to you. Properly used, the topic opener is a powerful technique for controlling the interview and learning how the person thinks.

11

Self-Appraisal Questions

*A common error is to allow the candidate to present only those facts about his past that he feels are relevant. . .. You, hopefully, will be a better judge of what is relevant, and so it is your task to elicit all of the information you will need to predict success.**

John Wareham
Secrets of a Corporate Headhunter

When candidates discuss various aspects of their background, facts come out that suggest behavioral traits. As an interviewer, one of our major challenges is to convert those facts into useful behavioral inferences.

Inferences about the candidate that can be made repeatedly during the interview form the basis for predicting on-the-job behavior.

DRAWING INFERENCES

Converting facts about someone into behavioral inferences is a key step in getting behind the resume. Too many interviewers over-

---

*John Wareham, excerpted from *Secrets of a Corporate Headhunter*. Copyright © 1980, The Wareham Family Trust. Reprinted with the permission of Atheneum Publishers.

look or fail to explore facts about candidates that can provide important insights into their potential for success. They accept facts for what they think they mean and then jump to conclusions that may not be true. For example, a candidate tells the interviewer he was president of his college fraternity. How is this fact relevant to the job for which the candidate is applying? Many interviewers might assume, perhaps accurately, that it indicates the candidate is a leader. But what kind of leader? A number of behavioral premises could explain this person's leadership qualities:

—team player   —bright
—well-liked   —enthusiastic
          —take-charge individual

How does an interviewer know which explanation is right? Which is the most reasonable behavioral inference? Perhaps all of them are right—or maybe none of them is. Behavioral interviewing will generate several inferences to explain a fact, but until interviewers know which inference is right, they can't predict on-the-job behavior.

The candidate will provide the meaning behind the fact if you ask the right question. The right question is a *Self-Appraisal Question*. This powerful technique, developed many years ago by an industrial psychologist, Dr. John Drake, has even greater usefulness today. The candidate's explanation of the fact or accomplishment is often situation-based and will help the interviewer decide if the candidate will fit the company, culture, and job situation. However, this requires proper development of the candidate/job profile outlined in Chapter 7 because that will set up the relevant behavioral factors that can be revealed by answers to Self-Appraisal Questions. Use of this question to verify your intuition is also now explained in Chapter 16.

Self-appraisal questions are easy to use. The interviewer takes a fact or accomplishment (such as the candidate's having been president of his college fraternity) and asks the candidate to tell something about himself based on that fact. "What would you say it was about you that led your fraternity brothers to select you as president?"

The candidate's answer will reflect his own assessment of why he was selected, and most likely something about the situation as

106

well. Here are a series of hypothetical answers. Note how each suggests one of the leadership qualities listed above:

1. "The house had two major factions, jocks and brains. I guess the fraternity brothers saw me as someone who could bridge both groups and get everyone together." *Behavioral inference: Team player.*

2. "I guess they saw me as pretty easygoing and someone who represented the house well on campus with many different people. I got along with everyone. Probably they wanted someone at that time who was very outgoing to represent our house. We needed more visibility on campus." *Behavioral inference: Well-liked.*

3. "Our house had just been placed on academic probation by the university. I had one of the best academic records in the house. My fraternity brothers thought I might be a model to others to get their grades up at a time when it was really important to do so." *Behavioral inference: Bright.*

4. "It was important that we do a good job in our next rush season and participate more actively as a house in intramural sports. I was always pretty enthused about things like that, so I guess that's why they picked me to be president." *Behavioral inference: Enthusiastic.*

5. "The house had suffered from having a very laid-back guy as the previous president. The place was getting run down, and the brothers were becoming undisciplined. They picked me probably because they knew I'd have clear goals and be forceful about how the house should be run." *Behavioral inference: Take-charge type.*

In each of these examples the Self-Appraisal Question enriches the interviewer's understanding of the candidate's leadership qualities and does so in a situational context.

If the job the candidate is now being considered for is a situation where strong leadership is sought, answer 5 suggests a much better candidate than does answer 2. If the organizational culture is one where being a good team player is more important than being bright, answer 1 is a better choice than answer 3. And so on.

In all cases, by asking a Self-Appraisal Question, you have gone far beyond what you might have inferred from the fact or accomplishment without the candidate's explanation. It is not enough to say the person is a leader. Interviewers need to know what kind of leader the candidate is and then relate that to their own hiring needs.

In fact, the candidate may not be a leader at all, even though he was a fraternity president:

> 6. "Why was I selected president of my fraternity? Simple. No one else wanted the job."

or

> 7. "My dad helped the house out of a major financial jam and bankrolled an expensive repair and refurbishing program. I guess my fraternity brothers picked me as president because they sort of felt they owed it to me."

The answers to Self-Appraisal Questions are the principal source from which inferences about the three Performance Factors are drawn and confirmed. In the example above, the first answer (team player) is an interpersonal quality; the third (bright) is an intellectual quality; and the fifth (take-charge individual) is motivational. Self-Appraisal Questions convert *what* someone did into an explanation of *how* it was done. They are the most powerful tool in behavioral interviewing.

CONFIRMING PREMISES

Getting answers to self-appraisal questions doesn't mean you have actually confirmed a behavioral inference. What you have done is let the candidate explain what he or she thinks a certain fact means. This is far preferable to relying on your own inference or conclusion. But before you can be sure that the inference is valid, you need to gather repeated evidence of that inference.

If a candidate seems to be enthusiastic—as evidenced by the reasons he stated for his selection as fraternity president—that is an inference that will need to be validated through several examples of his behavior. Otherwise you do not have a confirmed premise about the person, but merely an explanation of behavior in a single situation. Applying the Interview Model to multiple topics will give you a variety of situations in which to listen for evidence of the same premise.

Some interviewers are reluctant to use the Self-Appraisal Question. They are afraid such questions will embarrass the candidate.

In truth, candidates are often surprised and pleased to have an opportunity to talk in personal terms about *how* they did something. Few interviewers give them this chance. Self-Appraisal Questions encourage elaboration. They also help interviewers who have had experiences similar to the candidate's to avoid using subtle put-downs such as, "Oh, I was president of my fraternity, too. Now tell me about. . .."

There is no right or wrong answer to a Self-Appraisal Question. What makes the answer "right" is what it tells you about the candidate and how you then feel the person will fit into the job or situation.

Interviewers can use Self-Appraisal Questions to gain behavioral inferences about any fact or accomplishment the candidate has mentioned. For instance, when interviewers use Self-Appraisal Questions to learn about a promotion, they can discover what circumstances surrounding the event help explain it. If the circumstances match those in the job to be filled, a premise can be drawn from past experience which will help predict future behavior in the new situation.

In the following sequence, see what behavioral inferences you would make from each of the three responses.

Fact: This is the youngest person to be selected a sales manager in the history of the territory.

Q. (Self-Appraisal)—Why, do you suppose, were you selected?

A.—I increased sales to my customers by 30 percent in the first 18 months after they hired me.

Q. (Self-Appraisal)—What was it about your performance that also made them think you'd be a good manager?

A1.—My sales territory was one of the worst, with lots of tough customers and ongoing hostility. I overcame this, brought them around, and even became friends with a couple of them. I guess they thought those skills would make me effective as manager of the whole territory.

A2.—I solved a problem for the company—one posed by a major competitive threat to us in the field. I analyzed why customers were trying their product and came up with some creative ways to hold our distribution and get customers to try us for a new use which neither company had been promoting before. I guess management wanted me to help other salesmen develop solutions to similar problems.

A3.—I tend to bring a lot of energy to my job, and I organize my time well. I started reaching customers we hardly ever called on and upped our call frequency. In my new territory, other salesmen were coasting—they brought me in as a new manager and wanted me to fire them up.

From the above series of answers, we can see that three very different situations affected the candidate's behavior: hostile customers, new competitive threat, unproductive sales calls. What the interviewer will have to predict is whether the candidate can achieve similar results under circumstances that may be present or may arise within the interviewer's organization.

The Self-Appraisal Question enables the interviewer to go beyond the obvious facts and gain valuable insights into a person's behavior as it relates to particular circumstances and situations.

IF THE CANDIDATE ISN'T RESPONDING

Here are a few final pointers on self-appraisal questions. If candidates seem to have difficulty answering the question, give them an example from an earlier answer to use as a model of how to respond. "When you developed that new program for your company, it seemed you were very enthusiastic about the work. What would you say it was about you that made this more recent accomplishment possible?"

If you get a very short answer, probe more deeply. If the candidate says, "I got the contract approved so quickly bcause I'm good at what I do," ask for some elaboration. "What are the things you would say you do especially well in your job?" Or if the answer had been "I was able to do it because I work hard," ask the candidate to explain what he or she means by working hard. If continued responses to Self-Appraisal Questions seem evasive or undernourished, use a third-party self-appraisal. "What would your boss say you did to get the contract approved so quickly? What strengths would she have noticed in your performance?"

One powerful use of the Self-Appraisal Question is in exploring goals statements of well-prepared candidates. Often, these goals statements have been rehearsed to the point of perfection and can be very difficult to explore. A technique that works is to say, "Those are very impressive goals. What is it about you that makes those goals so appropriate for your career?" By phrasing a question this way, the interviewer requires the candidate to relate a goals statement (which may have been memorized from a book) to his or her own interests, priorities, motivation, and the like. Inability to do this may suggest the candidate is not really committed to the goals he claims. A Self-Appraisal Question can reveal this lack of motivation.

When candidates have described a string of accomplishments during the interview, applying Self-Appraisal Questions can reveal inconsistencies in their answers. If candidates read in your recruiting materials that your company is staffed with "creative, can-do" people, they may decide to convince you during the interview that they are "can-do" people, too. Self-Appraisal Questions will make it difficult and perhaps impossible for them to explain all their accomplishments this way if "creative" or "can-do" is not their natural style. You'll observe that although candidates may claim to be creative and "can-do," what you learn from the self-appraisal of their accomplishments is inconsistent with these qualities.

Finally, Self-Appraisal Questions can earn respect for you and your company for the way you interview. One loan officer from a large bank remembered these questions from her rounds of interviews when she received her MBA. She said only one interviewer of the dozens she encountered ever used this technique. She respected him because "It was the only question asked of me that really made me think."

SUMMARY

The Self-Appraisal Question is the most powerful tool interviewers have for getting behind the resume and learning more about the Performance Factors. Because it requires the candidate to explain the *how* of certain facts and accomplishments, it gives valuable insights into candidates' behavior and past performance. Answers to Self-Appraisal Questions provide essential information in the formation of behavioral premises about a candidate and their potential fit in a new job situation. The Self-Appraisal Question is the keystone of the Interview Model.

12

Situation-Based Questions

Before you begin interviewing . . . you must write out your entire interview presentation, plus write out potential responses to every conceivable situation.*

Stephen Merman and John McLaughlin
Outinterviewing the Interviewer

S ituation-Based Questions complete the Interview Model and provide an opportunity for the interviewer to learn how candidates perform in specific situations. The books on interviewing read by today's candidates contain lists of generic Situation-Based Questions, and well-prepared candidates are usually adept at answering them in an interview. Therefore, to be truly effective in getting behind the resume, these questions should be tailored as much as possible to situations that are likely to occur in the job you are trying to fill. They should also be carefully phrased so they don't reveal the answer you hope to hear. When developed and applied correctly, Situation-Based Questions are extremely valuable for determining whether the candidate will fit into your company, culture, and work environment.

---

*Stephen K. Merman and John E. McLaughlin, *Outinterviewing the Interviewer*, pp. 127, 135. (Englewood Cliffs, NJ: Prentice Hall, Inc., 1983).

Situation-Based Questions add variety to the interview and are excellent tools for getting behind the resume. There are four types:

- Problem Situation
- Continuum
- Comparison
- Future Assessment

In this chapter, each type of Situation-Based Question will be discussed. Multiple examples are provided so you can recognize each type and have a basis for creating any of them within the interviews you conduct. There are additional examples in Chapter 31. These should increase your comfort level with each type of question and add to your confidence so you can use your own situation-based questions to enliven and sharpen your interviews.

PROBLEM SITUATION

Problem Situation questions present candidates with a problem to be solved. The problem can represent something they encountered in their previous job(s) and should be something they are likely to run into in your company or department. Here's a question based on a problem situation that everyone has probably experienced: "Were you ever in a situation where you had too many things to do in the time available? How did you handle it?"

What you want to learn is how candidates manage their time: how they set goals and timetables, what *they* consider too much to do, and when and where they turn for help.

Another question might be "What if you worked for two supervisors and both gave you the same deadline for their project—if it became likely you could not satisfy both, how would you handle this problem?"

Here are more examples:

- "Have you ever had a problem where you had to handle an angry customer? What happened? How did you handle it?"

- "Imagine a situation where you find yourself without the specific technical knowledge to perform a task essential to a project. What would you do?"

- "Imagine you are asked to set up a task force to investigate the advantages of using temporary office workers in your company. If there were no precedent for establishing such a task force, how would you do it?"

- "Describe a work-related problem or situation in which you lost your temper. What happened and what were the results?"

- "If you had to interview someone for a position on your staff, and you lacked the technical depth to understand their competence, how would you handle the interview?"

Before your next interview, develop a list of such situations that are appropriate to your organization or work group. Then, ask candidates to tell how they would solve one or more of these problems. If they say they were never in such a situation, ask them to imagine they were and tell how they would handle it. You will find this a powerful technique to read problem solving skills of the candidate.

CONTINUUM

Continuum questions ask candidates to self-assess, using two positive qualities as points of reference. At least one of the attributes is important in the company, but not obviously so: "Where would you place yourself on a continuum from conceptual thinker to pragmatic executor?"

If you receive a guarded answer—"Oh, I'd be 50/50"—ask the candidate to pick one over the other. Say to the candidate, "No one is really right in the middle—wouldn't you be 60/40 or 30/70?" Whatever the response to your follow-up question, ask the candidate to explain how he or she chose that place on the continuum.

When constructing continuum questions, use positive and relatively equal values. If you ask candidates to place themselves on a continuum from being highly energetic to being extremely lazy, you'll get predictable answers!

Here are additional continuum questions:

● "How would you describe the energy you have as a point on a continuum: would it be marshalled intensively for specific projects or applied evenly across everything you do?"

● "Let's imagine you came as an outsider into a department with high turnover and lots of problems that you had to solve. If the decisions you made were placed on a continuum, would you prefer them to be right or well-liked?"

● "People tend to have one of two different styles in managing others: telling or selling. On a continuum with telling at one end and selling at the other, how would you say you work with others to get results?"

● "When you think back on a successful decision, do you tend to reflect on what was right about it or what could be improved?"

COMPARISON

Comparison questions ask candidates to compare two different situations, one of which is important to the job you have to fill. It is important not to signal to the candidate which situation relates to the job. Because you know the job situation, and the candidate doesn't, this question can be useful in gaining objective evaluations of candidates.

You can say to a candidate, "Please compare working for a boss whose strength is technical skills with working for a boss whose strength is managing and delegating the work of others." The response you receive helps you assess the candidate's potential for success, because you know the supervisory style of the person the candidate would be working for. It is important in posing a comparison question not to telegraph the more favorable answer. Do not say, "The person you would be working for is the kind of manager who is high on technical skills and not very good at delegating. Do you think you could work for someone like that?" If the candidate wants the job badly enough, he or she will say yes.

This next example describes two possible ways a new employee will be trained on the job (in this case, in a law firm): "Please compare these two situations where, as a new associate, you are being trained to take depositions. In one firm you have several days of training and role-playing. By the end of the week, you go out and take an actual deposition by yourself. In another firm, you accompany an attorney while he takes a deposition. You discuss it afterwards with him; then you take a number of them completely on your own throughout the rest of the week. What is it about one procedure that would make you prefer it over the other?"

For a clerical position you might ask: "Would you prefer a job with a few big projects to concentrate on and not much people contact, or one with many smaller tasks, lots of people contact, but frequent interruptions? Please compare how you would feel about these two situations, and in which you feel you would be more successful."

The comparison model is also a useful way to probe the candidate's practical knowledge of the job.

Imagine you are considering someone with a consumer packaged-goods marketing background for a new position marketing financial services in a bank. You can probe experience transferability with this question: "Please compare and contrast the marketing of packaged goods with the marketing of financial services." This question places the burden of assessing experience in a related but different field *on the candidate* and allows you to evaluate the candidate's understanding of both fields and his or her ability to point out the similarities and differences. It is also an effective device for probing a candidate's knowledge about a field without asking an awkward question such as, "What do you know about the marketing of financial services?"

If you have done your interview preparation, you will find these comparison questions useful for considering a candidate's likely fit with your culture and work environment. Here are three more comparison questions:

- "How would you compare your career progress to date with your expectations when you started this job/career?"

- "How would you compare and contrast your ability to handle a new project in these two different situations?" The first is where you receive a great deal of feedback and supervision and the second is where you have to figure it out for yourself and try your own approach."

● "Think for a minute about your current job compared with the one we are considering you for here. How would you compare and contrast your current job and this job in terms of challenge, satisfaction, and opportunity for success?"

FUTURE ASSESSMENT

Future assessment questions can reveal a great deal about how well candidates understand what is expected on the job and how they think they will do. When people talk about the future, they tend to be less guarded than when talking about current or previous work.

You can ask a candidate, "Let's imagine we hired you. It's a year from now and you are sitting down with your boss for your first formal performance evaluation. What would your boss say you'd done well, and in what areas would he or she be looking for more from you?"

Some other future assessment questions:

● "Does your present employer know you are looking for a new position? If so, what has been the reaction? If not, what is that reaction likely to be?

● "Let's say it's a year from now and you've compiled a successful record with us. How much would you attribute to the knowledge you brought into the job, and how much would be due to what you have learned from others since you've been here?"

● "If I met you again three years from now and you were disappointed in your progress with us, what might be some of the reasons for that?"

● "Do you have plans to continue your education in the future?"

● "What is you future career strategy?"

SUMMARY

Situation-Based Questions are vital to the successful application of the Interview Model. They allow you to focus, explore, refine, and confirm information that you have gathered through the other questioning techniques. The value of Situation-Based Questions is that they add variety and life to the interview while giving you the opportunity to evaluate the candidate against specific situations that are important to the job, your organization, and your organizational culture.

They will also help you collect examples that support inferences about the candidate's Performance Factors, particularly the Intellectual Factor. Because these questions are open-ended, they call for the conceptual responses from candidates. Situation-based

INTERVIEW MODEL

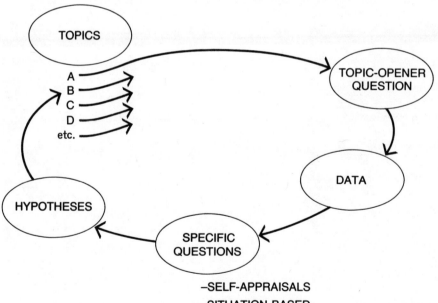

questions require you to apply many of the techniques considered thus far in the book, and they will help you keep control of the interview.

The power of the Interview Model depends on the appropriate use of these basic question types: Topic-Opener, Self-Appraisal, and Situation-Based. However, the key to gaining the most from any interview you conduct is how well you listen. The next chapter will examine listening skills and how they relate to interviewing.

13

Listening to What You Hear In the Interview

Listening, at least listening with understanding, is more than just sitting back and letting words flow into your ears. It is an active skill, at least as hard as talking—maybe harder. *

William N. Yeomans
1000 Things You Never Learned in Business School

None of what has been described so far will work unless interviewers are willing to listen. The Interview Model and its principal questioning techniques derive their value from the fact that a few short, open-ended questions ("Tell me about your college years") can evoke longer and more thoughtful answers than a series of detailed questions that prescribe what a candidate must include in the answer.

Behavioral interviewing is based on the belief that if you hear enough examples of a candidate's behavior you will be able to predict the qualities that the candidate draws on and then predict his or her potential for success. To hear all of this requires listening. The advice

---

*William N. Yeomans, *1000 Things You Never Learned in Business School* (New York: New American Library, 1984).

we give our clients is that interviewers should listen 80 percent of the time. We also remind them that they have two ears and one mouth, and should remember that ratio when conducting an interview!

Good listeners encourage others to talk. Interviewers who are good listeners learn more about candidates than those who are not. They also maintain more effective control of the interview process. Skeptics may question that statement. It would seem to some that the person who is talking is the one in control. Not so. Today's candidates are coached in ways to get interviewers talking about themselves and their organizations. When you prevent that from happening in the interviews you conduct, you stay in control. When a candidate gets you to do all the talking, then it is you, not the candidate, who is being interviewed.

ACTIVE LISTENING

The concept of "active listening," used widely in counseling, has some application in the interview process as well. In this process, you "listen with the third ear" for what the candidate is really saying. In behavioral interviewing, this is particularly important when gathering evidence about the Performance Factors. When you listen actively, you pick up important signals to follow up on in later questions. Listening to what you hear can lead you to a better understanding of the candidate's intellectual, interpersonal, and motivational factors.

Demonstrate Acceptance

While the candidate is talking, you should give nonverbal signs of acceptance. Nod your head, smile, maintain a relaxed posture, etc. This keeps the interview flowing. Acceptance does not mean agreement. Even if you don't like what the candidate is saying, you should listen openly. By doing so, you will hear a great deal. Other acceptance techniques are discussed in Chapter 9, *Setting a Mood for the Interview.*

Summarize

When the interviewee finishes an answer, you can follow up with a question that summarizes what has just been said. This technique lets the candidate know you have been listening. It can also let the candidate know that you want more information or verification of what has just been said. "I heard you to say a few moments ago that it would not be a problem for you and your family to move here from California. Did I understand you correctly?" You are probing the candidate's mobility as a key factor in motivation. The candidate knows by your response that you have heard something *not* said: hesitance, perhaps, or uncertainty. The candidate will now have to verify to your satisfaction that moving would not be a problem.

Rephrase

Another way to return to the candidate's answer and gain more information is to say, "Are you saying, then, that if you had the choice between working for a boss who supervised you closely or one who trusted you to be on your own, that you would prefer to be left on your own?" This will give the candidate an opportunity to elaborate further. You might even ask a Self-Appraisal Question here: "What is it about you that makes you prefer to work for a boss with that style?" A third type of lead-in that shows you have been listening is, "Do you mean, then, that while you were with United Corporation you were responsible for developing an entirely new accounts receivable system? Tell me more about that."

More Than Mere Words

Active listening can also uncover concerns about the candidate. Certain repeated evidence of performance or values which run counter to the organization's culture will occur when you listen to many examples of the candidate's behavior on the job or in school. It may be in what the candidate says; it also may be in the way it's said. You may detect signs or a pattern of cynicism, hostility, indecisiveness, or other qualities which would make the candidate unsuitable for this position.

Active listening can also uncover the subtle underpinnings of this person's potential for success. Interviewees may offer repeated instances of enthusiasm, problem-solving, self-starting ability and creativity that will lead you to a decision that this person is exactly the right person for the job.

LISTENING AND THE INTERVIEW MODEL

At the outset, the interviewer should create an interview climate that is nonthreatening and conducive to listening. The small talk that precedes an interview should be an easy conversational exchange that is shared fairly equally between the interviewer and the candidate.

The actual interview begins with an opening statement. This gives a clear signal to the candidate that it's time to get on with the purpose of the meeting. At this point, control should shift firmly to the interviewer. The candidate should be told that he or she is going to be doing most of the talking while the interviewer listens and takes notes. Sticking to these ground rules is important to the outcome of the interview.

The Topic-Opener Question provides an excellent opportunity for the interviewer to listen. In fact, the effect of this questioning technique is diminished by interruptions. As you listen and take notes, you will be hearing more than just the answer to your question. You will also be hearing how well the candidate organizes and selects information for the answer and expresses his or her thoughts. If, for instance, you ask the candidate to tell you about his current job, you may hear more than what the candidate is telling you.

"Well, at the beginning of this job I thought it was going to be great. It seemed like just the place I wanted to be. I liked the people I worked with and we all got along just great. But the work . . . I don't know . . . it just didn't turn out to be what I wanted it to be. I thought I'd have opportunities to be creative and do some of my own projects, but it seemed like all I did was other people's work. I really have a lot to offer an organization, but somehow I just haven't been able to get it across where I am right now. No matter how well I do, it seems like I am not moving up. I want to move up in an organization, so I'm looking for another opportunity. Some of the other people in my work group feel the same way. They agree with me that I'm probably not in the right place now and should try to get somewhere where I can be appreciated and receive recognition."

Here are some facts that can be heard, although the candidate did not state them directly.

1. His choice of information about his current job focused entirely on how it had not worked out. It is as though the question was "Tell me why you are leaving your current job."

2. Although the question asked the candidate to describe the *job*, his first words were about the people he worked with rather than the work. This could indicate that the social aspect of the work was more interesting than the work itself.

3. Although the job didn't turn out to be what the candidate wanted it to be, the interviewer is given no clues about what the person was looking for. This is a good indication that maybe he still doesn't know what he is looking for.

4. The candidate sounds like a complainer, and the fact that the members of his work team are aware of his dissatisfaction indicates that he may also be a gossip.

5. The answer lacks specifics. The candidate has answered in generalizations, which may indicate difficulty in expressing thoughts explicitly.

To be fair, some of the candidate's statements deserve further explanation. A follow-up question might gain understanding into what exactly he expected in his current job. "You mentioned just now that the job has not turned out to be what you expected. Tell me more about that."

"Well, I remember that when the job was posted—I was already working for the company—it mentioned there would be opportunities for working independently on projects. After I got the job, I found out that this project work was in addition to what I was doing already, and I didn't feel like they had explained that the workload was going to be so heavy. So I tried to do some of these extra projects, but none of them seemed to impress my boss. I gave up doing them—it didn't matter to the job—but I sure hated to miss the chance to move ahead that those who did the projects received."

A number of behavioral clues are gained by really listening to this answer. First of all, the candidate obviously didn't ask questions about the job before he accepted it. This is consistent with his lack of understanding of the job expressed in the first answer. Secondly, the fact that this project work was clearly part of an incentive program for those interested in advancement (and perhaps financial reward) was not enough motivation for him to put in the extra hours. The good listener will pick up significant clues about drive, ambition, and interests. He also evidences a lack of persistence: The first few projects did not impress anyone, so he gave up.

Contrast that exchange with the following Topic Opener and response:

Interviewer: Tell me about your current job.

Candidate (takes time to think): I believe the most rewarding part of my current job is that I'm part of a cohesive work group and yet, at the same time, have an opportunity—through an employee incentive program—to develop projects independently for review by my supervisor. Although this means I sometimes put in fairly long hours, the rewards really make up for it. I'm learning so much about the job that I'm in and about my potential to do more—and perhaps eventually to supervise projects.

What you hear in the second answer is vastly different from what is heard in the first, yet it describes the same entry on a resume: Member, Project Team. Listening is an essential skill for getting behind the resume.

As you implement the Interview Model, you will find that listening also helps you evaluate responses to Self-Appraisal Questions. In the second response above, assume the candidate went on to describe a particular project that he had completed that was well-received by his supervisor. A Self-Appraisal Question would help you better understand what this meant to the candidate, and would give you clues to his motivation.

Interviewer: You mentioned earlier that one of the projects you completed was very favorably evaluated by your supervisor. That's very impressive. What do you think it was about your work on the project that led to recognition by your supervisor?

Candidate (thinks): I believe it was that I did all the original research on my own—and on my own time. Data gathering is something I really enjoy, and so it was no problem for me to spend time after work going through reports and extracting the information I needed. The conclusions I drew from the program were well-substantiated by previous data from the company, and I think they were surprised and pleased that I had taken the extra effort to go back through related documents and data. The recognition I received was actually from my work group, because the project was related to some issues we had been dealing with. My supervisor saw to it that I got the promised bonus, but for me the really great part of it was the support and praise of my co-workers.

This answer provides rich data for the interviewer who really listens. What the interviewer hears is evidence of Performance Factors: analytical, thorough, self-starting, hard-working, peer-oriented. Additionally, the way in which the candidate expressed this answer provides more support for a growing premise about the person's ability to express himself. "Articulate" and "thoughtful" could be added to the quickly growing list of adjectives that are beginning to describe this candidate.

Listening also is key in the analysis of answers to Situation-Based Questions. One of the things to listen for is how well the candidate's answers to these hypothetical or actual problem situations match what you have already heard in earlier answers about how they deal with problems. It is yet another way of getting behind the resume: Are candidates telling you what they think you want to hear, or are they telling you what they actually would do or have done?

Go back to the first candidate in the example above. Imagine that you asked the following Comparison Question: "If you had a choice of two different bosses to work for—one who gave you a few directions and more or less put you on your own and one who preferred to supervise closely—with which do you think you would be most successful?"

If the candidate responds, "I think I'd be more successful with the one who let me work on my own, because I really like to have my own assignments and do them independently," you are hearing the answer he thinks you want to hear or the one he wants to be true.

Remember what you heard in his response to the Topic Opener Question about his job. You heard his own description of how he eventually gave up trying to do projects independently when he didn't receive the kind of feedback he wanted. If there has been other evidence in his answers that he works better with supervision than without it, you may wish to follow up on this apparent discrepancy by asking a question which will introduce stress, a topic covered in Chapter 15.

You can say to the candidate, "I am surprised that you feel you would be more successful in the situation where there is little supervision. Several examples you have given me from your current job indicate to me that you in fact don't do as well when you have to work independently. Can you tell me more about why you think you would be more successful with a boss like that?"

The candidate's response to this question may tell you a great deal about his motivation, frustrations, and limitations. "Well, I've always thought I would work better on my own. I guess I was thinking of an ideal situation when you asked the question. I've always dreamed of being a project leader, responsible for the data gathering and for the program . . . but every time I get close to a situation like that I just don't seem to make it. It seems like I need the supervision to get things done, but I don't really like being supervised. I don't know . . . I just never seem to get that extra encouragement when I need it the most."

By actively listening to this answer, you learn that the candidate is externally rather than internally motivated. To be productive he needs a set of clearly defined objectives and a supervisor who not only will see that he gets his work done, but perhaps will find ways to help him be more independent. If this isn't possible in the job situation for which he is interviewing, then the organization should not hire him.

Listening for Unspoken Messages

Listening is critical to the success of the behavioral interviewing process, and sometimes what you *don't* hear is as important as what you *do* hear. This is particularly true when a candidate is describing accomplishments. In Chapter 14, techniques for probing accomplishments are discussed, but their effectiveness depends on how well you hear what the candidate is saying.

If a candidate is describing the development of a new system evaluation process as an accomplishment of which she is proud, listen for how she describes her role. If she is vague, or uses "we" more than "I," listen to what she may *not* be saying: that her role was actually rather limited, and the accomplishment really can't be claimed by her alone.

SUMMARY

Active listening in an interview enhances the formation of behavioral premises about the candidate. When you interview, you should have in mind the Performance Factors from the candidate/job profile, and listen for repeated evidence of behavior that indicates the presence of these qualities. Active listening will allow you to make a great many inferences about the candidate, which then can be translated into qualities which will compare favorably or unfavorably with those on the candidate/job profile. From this process, a better hiring decision will be made.

14

Probing Accomplishments and Limitations

*Honesty in an interview consists basically of three elements: truth, consistency, and candor.**

H. Anthony Medley
Sweaty Palms: The Neglected Art of Being Interviewed

T o be revealing and effective, an interview must cover the candidate's accomplishments *and* limitations. Along with specifics claimed under the Resume Factor, these two topics are the ones where candidates are most likely to consider stretching the truth. Candidates want to look good, and they want to downplay their limitations. Therefore, unless you are willing to probe stated accomplishments and get the candidate to talk about job-related limitations, you will not have a complete and accurate picture of the person you are interviewing.

Applicants do not tend to lie during an interview, but they have been known to omit facts or imply positive things in order to leave a favorable impression—especially when they start describing various

---

*H. Anthony Medley, *Sweaty Palms: The Neglected Art of Being Interviewed* (Berkeley, CA: Ten Speed Press, 1984).

accomplishments. Likewise, most candidates won't willingly discuss their limitations—and most interviewers are reluctant to bring them up. The techniques described in this chapter will help you comfortably explore both of these sensitive areas. Success in probing both areas in your interviews will enrich the value of subsequent reference checks and give you more confidence that you have a balanced picture of the candidate when you are ready to make a decision.

PROBING ACCOMPLISHMENTS

The purpose of probing accomplishments is to find out whether candidates are results-oriented. Are their accomplishments an important part of the way they think about their jobs and what they do? When they talk about their careers to date, do they describe their careers in terms of accomplishments? Or do they describe them more in terms of positions and titles?

Results-oriented people remember their accomplishments. They are proud of them and willing to talk about a number of specifics related to these accomplishments. As you listen to what they say, you will want to know not only *what* they accomplished but *how* they did it.

If candidates can explain how they accomplished what they did, the chances are that they really did perform as well as they claim—and perhaps could have similar successes for your company. The corollary to this principle is if they can't give you details about how they accomplished something, the chances are they did not play a large role in the event—or perhaps it was not their responsibility at all.

The sequence of probing begins with a Topic Opener question: "Tell me about a recent accomplishment you're proud of." Once an applicant names a specific accomplishment, you should begin to ask for specifics: "Could you tell me step by step how you did this?" "What was your role in it?" "What problems came up that you were required to handle, and how did you handle them?"

If you find an applicant describing his or her accomplishments in general terms and appearing uncomfortable in providing much detail, you may observe that he or she begins to use the word *we* a great deal: "we analyzed . . ., we recommended . . ., we suggested that . . ., we improved. . . ."

As you listen, you probably will want more specific details about the candidate's role in this accomplishment. Ask for them! Ask the person to replace the word *we* with the word *I*: "What you're describing is very interesting, but I'd like to know more about *your* role in this accomplishment. Could you describe again what you did, but this time replace 'we' with 'I'?"

If you intend to do follow-up reference checks, you should also ask candidates to tell you to whom they reported during this project. If they reply, "Well, the department manager" or "my boss" or "the supervisor," ask for the person's name. Then ask if that person is listed among the candidate's references. If not, ask if that person can be added to the list. There are three reasons for doing this:

• Asking for specific names suggests you may follow up and check on what candidates are telling you. This encourages candor on their part.

• This list of names will be useful if you decide to confirm with previous employers that the candidates really accomplished what they've claimed. It's often difficult, if not impossible, to find out who a given supervisor was two or three years ago unless you get the person's name during the interview.

• You want to see if the people mentioned in connection with this accomplishment are already among the references or can be added. If the candidate is reluctant to have you talk with a former supervisor, you'll want to know why.

When you hear accomplishments in this detail, you may run across a partial accomplishment. This requires your careful listening and further probing. For instance, an associate partner in a law firm involved in a merger-and-acquisition deal may describe her role in the following terms: "I took the lead in getting the work done and out of our firm. I was the one person from the firm who was consistently in on this deal. I was the lead associate on it."

But what the attorney *hasn't* said is whether she did any negotiating in this process. If you've listened carefully to her description, and if you know your business, you'll want to follow up and ask if her role also involved handling some of the negotiating. If not, that doesn't necessarily mean she wasn't the "lead associate," merely that the accomplishment wasn't completely or fully hers. Although she oversaw the work, she did not handle one of the key aspects of the deal—the negotiation itself.

Sometimes it's useful to probe accomplishments by setting the question in the future, and in your own company. This is an excellent chance to get a reading on how a candidate's way of achieving results will mesh with your particular corporate environment.

For example, I've heard an executive search professional ask a candidate for a senior marketing position in a manufacturing company, "What makes you think you can introduce a new marketing strategy into the company when they have a tradition of changing much more slowly than your current employer?" This is an effective way to get a reading on someone's ability to achieve an expected future accomplishment, given the impact of the company's culture.

Here is another example from the same executive search professional: "As the new Human Resources Director, you'll have to introduce new policies without upsetting the more senior managers in this company. What makes you think you could pull that off successfully?" Again, the question effectively blends the realities of the job situation and the culture of the company with the candidate's anticipated ability to perform in the future.

Cautions When Considering Work Samples

There are some positions where applicants can bring in samples of their work as evidence of accomplishments. But here, the interviewer can run into problems. One is the question of authorship: Is the work you're being shown *really* the work of the individual you are interviewing or someone else's? Rather than flatly questioning if applicants really did their work, you can subtly probe the credibility of what you're hearing or seeing. If the person claims development of an advertisement or campaign for a client, ask: "What alternatives did you consider and reject before deciding on this one? Also, how did you decide this was the right one to go with?" Or, "What was the client's reaction when you presented your ideas— were they quickly accepted or did it take several meetings?"

I have also heard an art director say to candidates, "These proofs are very impressive, but I'd also like to see some roughs that were turned down by clients and yet are still among your proudest accomplishments." Here, the interviewer recognized that while people do steal proofs, they seldom steal rough layouts. And layouts that a person thinks are terrific are good evidence of how that person thinks and what kind of work that person will do on the job and be proud of.

A second problem is that inexperienced candidates trying to enter a field may not yet have relevant samples of work to show you. The creative director in one advertising agency says to young people who have no portfolio, "Look, I'd like to see the way you think about creating advertising and advertising campaigns. If you'd like to talk further with me, why don't you go through some magazines in the next few days and pick out five *bad* advertisements as you see them. When you come in again, tell me what you would do to make them good or more effective advertising. Similarly, I would like you to pick five good ads and create the next ad in the same campaigns. In other words, show me how you would expand the ads you selected into a campaign theme."

How Self-Appraisal Questions Help

One of the most effective ways to go from the *what* to the *how* when understanding an accomplishment is to use Self-Appraisal Questions. "That's a very impressive accomplishment. Tell me, what was it about you that enabled you to be so successful in that project?"

Sometimes, when hearing about an accomplishment, it is hard to relate to the candidate's enthusiasm and pride. Perhaps the deed has been only briefly described or falls outside your area of expertise. Or maybe it was accomplished in an environment that is unfamiliar to you, making it difficult to appreciate. A Self-Appraisal Question can help here, too. Consider the following exchange:

Interviewer: Tell me about a recent accomplishment you are particularly proud of.

Candidate: We created a new employment system that managers can use on their own to complete a requisition or source candidate "profiles."

Interviewer: (asking for clarification on this seemingly routine accomplishment): What is it about that new employment system that makes you especially proud?

Candidate: Oh, we made it available on floppy disks so we now have a virtually paperless employment system in our company.

Probing accomplishments will give you a much more complete picture of the candidate, and heighten your understanding of what the candidate can contribute to your organization. Similarly, what you will learn about a candidate when you probe limitations will increase your confidence that you have adequate information about a candidate to make a good hiring decision.

PROBING LIMITATIONS

Many interviewers choose not to probe for limitations. They feel it will change the friendly nature of the interview, making the applicant feel uncomfortable. This is a major mistake. It's as important to understand people's limitations as it is to understand their strengths. While some candidates are open about disclosing their shortcomings during one interview, most are not.

When you're interviewing candidates, one thing to recognize is that admitting errors is really a sign of strength rather than weakness. Competent, successful, self-confident people are willing to acknowledge some things they don't do quite so well. In response to "What are some parts of your job that you don't feel you handle as well as other parts?" you might get as an answer, "Well, I'm not very good at strategic planning, so long-range strategy is not one of my strengths."

Your next question: "Well, what do you do to overcome that?" Answer: "Well, I tend to surround myself with people who *are* good at strategic planning."

In short, successful people not only know what their limitations are, they have found ways to compensate for them. If you interview a candidate who has *no* limitations, shortcomings, or weaknesses, this doesn't mean you've found the ideal candidate! Instead, it probably means you simply haven't probed deeply enough during the interview.

If the first and major portion of an interview has focused on accomplishments, it's relatively easy to explore a candidate's limitations—without destroying the constructive climate of the interview. A key strategy in probing limitations is to refer to them always as "limitations" or "areas for improvement"—not as "weaknesses."

>>>**IS THE GRASS REALLY GREENER?**→ One of the paradoxes interviewers face is that people from the outside often look better than current employees. The reason for this is that we know our own people's limitations. When interviewing external candidates, it's far more difficult to find out what their shortcomings are. And yet it's important to do so.

Questions that probe for limitations are most effective when introduced about three-quarters of the way through the interview. Most candidates find it difficult to praise themselves throughout an entire interview. Our experience is that if you give them ample opportunity to talk about their successes, they may be more willing to share some of their shortcomings.

One bridge to this side of the interview is to say, "You've got many strengths as they relate to this job, but everyone has limitations, too. What are the things you don't do quite so well?"

Chances are that any immediate answer to this question will not reveal much about the candidate's limitations. But you can use several levels of probes to get at this information.

At the *first level*, many candidates are prepared for a question like, "What, would you say, are your limitations or shortcomings?" In response, they may deny that they have any limitations or shortcomings. They'll give you an answer like, "Well, I just don't have any major limitations" or "There's nothing particular I can point to. Anything I don't do well, I work extra hard to improve."

They may also try to pass off an asset or positive quality in the guise of a limitation by saying, "Well, I tend to set standards for myself that are really high," or "I tend to be a perfectionist," or "I tend to work almost too hard at everything I do." These are nonanswers. The candidates are trying to slip another positive attribute past you rather than stating a limitation.

Don't let candidates hand you positives as limitations. If you hear "I set high standards" in response to your question about what might be improved in their work, you should respond by saying, "I'm puzzled why you would name setting high standards as a negative. I'm interested in why you feel that's a shortcoming. Tell me more." This usually gets the candidate back on track and produces a more thoughtful and honest answer.

See how these two answers to the interviewer's question above provide clues to the candidate's behavioral qualities:

● "Well, in my current company I'm surrounded by mediocre people, so I'm looking to change to a company where most of the people will work at my high level."

● "Setting high standards becomes a problem when I can't accept things at a 90 percent level and will border on perfectionism when it's not called for."

The first respondent's arrogance, not his or her high standards, may be the *real* limitation!

If you run into either a denial of any shortcomings or the "positive, but let's pretend it's a negative" nonanswer, you may want to say, "Well, I recognize you may not have any *major* shortcomings—you are a very accomplished person. But what are a couple of areas where you feel improvement is still possible?"

With this technique, you've narrowed the frame of the discussion, and candidates may feel less threatened. They may be prompted to name some small quality that they could still improve upon. Or they may try a different response. They will acknowledge a limitation, but then quickly tell you what they've done about it so it no longer exists. This strategy follows advice to candidates in books about interviewing. Here is an example, from *Outinterviewing the Interviewer*, of how to respond to such questions:

"One specific area is that I need to learn to delegate better. To correct this I have done some of my own professional development through modeling others and attending a seminar on effective delegation."

To counter this "here is a problem but I've already solved it" response, ask, "What still needs improvement in your ability to delegate?" or "That's commendable, but I'm still interested in learning about other areas where you feel improvement could occur."

Even at this juncture, many applicants are unwilling to admit their limitations. If you still get resistance at this point, then shift to the past tense and ask: "We all tend to grow and change over the years. As you consider former limitations, how would you say you have grown and developed the most?" This change in tense implies you are looking for something that used to be a problem but is now in the past.

Candidates may now finally name a limitation they are trying to overcome. At this point, even the most arrogant candidates will feel a little foolish at having absolutely *no* shortcomings to disclose. Because of the way you phrase the question, suggesting that it was a *previous* problem that no longer counts against them, they may feel safe to discuss it with you.

In response, you might get a statement something like the following: "Well, I used to lose my temper with dumb clients in meetings. I used to interrupt them and cut them short, but I don't have that problem anymore." Candidates may even think their "victory" is a positive step—but the chances are they're telling you something that still is a shortcoming or limitation.

Once a "previous" limitation is revealed, it is important to satisfy yourself that the candidate has indeed grown beyond it. Going back to the previous example, continue the questioning:

"What made you decide to stop interrupting clients in meetings?" Then, "How did you bring yourself around to this change in behavior?"

If you're not convinced that the behavior has changed, ask the candidate to describe a recent meeting or situation where he or she was tempted to interrupt but didn't.

In addition to the techniques mentioned above, there are several other strategies you can use for probing limitations.

Get a Third-Party Viewpoint

Ask the candidate to describe herself or himself from a third-party standpoint. For example, "If I called your boss, how would he or she describe your work as a territory manager during the last few years?"

If the response you get is filled only with positives and praise, with no indication of any limitations, hold the answer up for the candidate to reexamine. Say something like the following: "Well, that's a very impressive profile. But if you worked for this person for two years, wouldn't he or she have seen *anything* that you don't do quite so well? Isn't there any area of improvement or development he could point to? This is a somewhat imbalanced picture you have given me of yourself."

Other third-party sources to use in this kind of probe include a major customer or client; anyone they currently supervise, a peer with whom they work, or, if the candidates are still students, a professor who knows them well.

A variation on this would be: "It sounds like your boss (key customer, etc.) is very pleased with your work. If she had one wish for you in terms of possible improvement, what would it be?" Of course, all of this cushions the discussion of limitations with positive qualities, thus increasing the likelihood that the candidate can be honest and not souring the tone of the interview.

Self-Ratings vs. Ratings by the Boss

Another technique for understanding limitations is one from a senior executive search professional. Her method blends several of the techniques presented in this book. It can yield a more objective assessment of claimed strengths, some of which may more accurately be described as limitations.

She begins her questioning by providing candidates with a list of four to six job-related strengths for self-assessment. For a sales manager these might include: motivating others, delegation, persuasiveness, competitive analysis, and sales forecasting. Then she asks the candidates to rate themselves on each factor using a scale of one to ten or one to five (where larger numbers equal higher ratings).

To complete this assessment, she asks each candidate, "On which factors would your boss rate you differently—either higher or lower?" (Note that she does *not* say, "How would your boss rate you on those same qualities?" The answer to that question would likely be, "The same way.")

Responses that name a higher rating by the boss suggest the candidate may have underrated his or her skills. Cases where the candidate thinks the boss would have given a lower rating invite a further probe: "You said your boss would actually rate you a little lower on delegation. What makes you think that?" Lower ratings by the boss may provide a more valid assessment of strengths than what the candidate claims.

>>>**SOFTEN PROBING QUESTIONS** → Probing for limitations is sometimes an uncomfortable exercise. If you don't want to confront the candidate too directly, you can soften your questions or statements. Phrases like these are good lead-ins: "I wonder if . . . (financial forecasting is a skill you will need to develop)" or "Do you suppose that . . .?" or "Would you say that . . .?" or "Is it possible that . . .?"

Focus on Development Needs

Another strategy for probing limitations is to focus on development needs. One way to do this is to pose a strength development question. This question builds on the idea that it is easier to talk about a current strength that requires future development than to discuss a strength that is lacking completely.

Pick a skill that is important on the job, such as making presentations, and put it into a strength development question: "Consider your skill in making presentations. Would you say it is a skill you are currently well satisfied with, or do you think it needs further strengthening?" Regardless of which choice the candidate makes, you can follow up with another question.

If the response indicates the candidate is satisfied, then ask a self-appraisal question: "What is it about your current skill in making presentations that has given you the feeling you do not need to strengthen it further?" If the candidate says that further strengthening is needed, ask, "What do you feel needs further strengthening?" You may hear an answer like the following: "I still need to improve

141

my ability to handle hostile questions" or "I need to be able to speak in front of a large group from a podium."

Another way to get candidates to focus on developmental needs is to say, "Imagine we hired you, brought you into our company, and made available to you an annual allowance of $750 to spend on any self-improvement program related to your job. In what kind of course do you think you would invest those dollars?" Answers might include the following: "Well, I'm not so comfortable with the financial side of the job, so I think I'd take one of those three-day courses in accounting for nonfinancial people" or "I'd like to get even better organized, so would like to try one of those time-management courses." Phrasing the question this way can help you open up a limitation area that hasn't been mentioned before.

If candidates refuse to name any limitations, ask them to rank order all their strengths. This should give you an idea of their range and relationship of strengths. The strengths that are omitted can also tell you a great deal. Let's say that ability to deal with stress is a quality you feel is needed for the job. When candidates rank order their strengths but fail to place "ability to deal with stress" high on the list (or don't name it at all), it may not be one of their strengths.

Always let candidates self-assess and name their own strengths first. If you offer a list from which to choose, you may telegraph your priorities. If a candidate omits a strength you are looking for, you can ask directly about it. Rank ordering is also a very effective technique for another reason: It forces the candidate to select and prioritize— giving you more direct input from the candidate on what is important.

To end this chapter on a positive note, I'd like to describe briefly a concept that may have a bearing on what you hear in an interview. *Sometimes, people's weaknesses are really their strengths carried to excess.*

What that means is that if people overuse a strength, it can become a limitation. Perhaps you've run into someone who's extremely analytical and overuses this strength with the result that he or she can't make a decision. Before he makes a recommendation, he needs "more data," "one more study," "one more piece of research." What he's stricken with is "analysis paralysis." An overused strength becomes a weakness.

In the same vein, an articulate person who overuses that strength becomes verbose and never stops talking.

I've also known decisive people who become stubborn and rigid under certain circumstances. From their lips flow statements like the following: "Don't confuse me with the facts, I've made up my mind" or "I don't want to discuss this any more. I've already made my decision."

One final example of strengths carried to excess thus becoming weaknesses: People who are too accommodating of others' requests can easily become overcommitted. I know people—as I am sure you do—who will promise that any number of projects can be completed by the end of the week, when in fact they already have more than can be comfortably handled.

Most commonly, people overuse their strengths when they're under pressure—when they change jobs or get a new supervisor, or when an associate leaves and they have to pick up the slack. A sudden crash deadline or a new customer to handle can produce stress on the job and make people want to look good. Naturally, they fall back on their strengths. But if they're under excessive stress, their judgment may be impaired to the point where they overdo it.

If you encounter some of these weaknesses in an interview, ask yourself: Are they really strengths carried to excess? You may want to relate them to their context, as possible confirmations of the strengths you've already started to hypothesize about this person. You'll also be getting important signals about what kind of job environment a person will work in successfully, without turning strengths into limitations.

Exploring limitations is as important as exploring strengths. While the task may seem unpleasant, it need not be. By setting an atmosphere of acceptance during the major portion of the interview you'll find that people will be willing to talk about the things they think they could do better—as well as the things they already do well.

SUMMARY

To get behind the resume, you must probe both accomplishments and limitations with all candidates. Only then will you have the balanced set of behavioral premises that you need to make the right hiring decision.

15

The Proper Use of Stress and Silence

Answer questions, not statements. If the employer comments about your background or experience, acknowledge the statement, and avoid adding information unless it is clearly called for, or in your best interest.*

Tom Jackson
Guerrilla Tactics in the Job Market

S tress and silence are powerful tools for the interview. There are proper ways to use these techniques during a behavioral interview. Because the success of this type of interviewing depends at least partly on the degree to which candidates feel acceptance, it's important to know the reasons and the right way to use stress, and when to use silence. Both of these techniques can become counterproductive if misused. There are techniques for using both that will help you conduct a revealing and productive interview.

STRESS AS AN INTERVIEW TECHNIQUE

The *Improper* Use of Stress

Stress interviews, in which candidates are placed under continuous and excessive pressure, are the antithesis of the kind of inter-

---

*Tom Jackson, *Guerrilla Tactics in the Job Market* (New York: Bantam Books, 1978).

145

viewing recommended in this book. Stress interviews are essentially interrogations. They begin and are carried on with questions like the following:

"You have a very unimpressive resume. Why should I even bother to conduct this interview?" or, "What are your major personal flaws that would get in the way of your accomplishing this job? List at least five of them" or, "Quick, give me a thirty-second commercial about yourself" or, "If you were going to describe yourself as any kind of an animal, what kind of an animal would you be and why?" We know of an interviewer with one organization who requested candidates to "Say something so funny it will make me laugh." The idea, of course, is to see how well applicants can think under pressure, or whether they will respond adversely to such questions.

Questions such as these do not generate behavioral premises that help you gain insights into a candidate's potential for success on the job. They are threatening to candidates, inhibit their responses, and can give candidates a poor impression of your organization.

Some interview situations can create stress and must be handled carefully. In Chapter 9, The Interview Model, panel interviews are described. These interviews—in which a number of interviewers meet with the candidate at the same time—require special techniques which are outlined in that chapter. In some organizations, the panel interview has been carried to excess. One of our clients regularly turned interviews into tribunals. They invited candidates to their offices after 6 p.m., then they brought them individually into a room with 12 to 18 people. Their rationale was that this did not tie up busy people during the day and it saved everyone's time. They failed to recognize how stressful this was for possibly superior candidates and what a turnoff it was to applicants seeking to learn more about the company and its culture.

We once consulted with a law firm that did extensive litigation work. The partners felt that their major task in an interview was to determine whether law students could fit into their high-pressure work environment. Accordingly, the firm arranged for their five most senior partners to sit in the firm's boardroom and brought students in one at a time for an "inquisition." They felt this was a good way to decide whom they were going to hire: A student who could survive tough questions from five litigators sitting around the table was probably a candidate who would succeed with their firm. But they began to question the effectiveness of this interviewing method when they found it more and more difficult to get candidates to accept the offers they were extending.

In other legendary variations of the stress-interview situation, there may be no ashtray for the smoker—or no furniture. The window is nailed shut, and the candidate has to open it. Admiral Hyman Rickover was reputed to have conducted interviews in which candidates were required to sit on a chair or stool whose front legs were several inches shorter than the rear ones.

The problem with conducting stress interviews is twofold. First, stress keeps the candidate from relaxing, feeling comfortable, and being willing to share information with you. Second, the major defense for conducting a stress interview—"We have a high-stress job, so we have to see if people can handle stress"—doesn't hold water. There is no established correlation between a candidate's ability to handle stress on the job and his or her ability to handle it in an interview that you conduct. And often, the stress interview is seen as play-acting. I know of one candidate who simply ignored an interviewer's rudeness, seeing how much of a fool the man would make of himself. After all, the applicant had nothing to lose, having already decided from the nature of the interview that this was not a good place to work.

When people recollect their experiences with "stress interviews," they invariably remember them as being awful. Even though the interviews occurred as many as ten years before, some survivors vow they still won't buy the products manufactured by companies with which they had stress interviews.

The *Proper* Use of Stress

While a stress *interview* is not recommended, in some situations it is appropriate to apply a little stress on the candidate. The right time is when you are in the latter stages of the interview, feel favorably disposed toward the candidate, but still have *an important unresolved conflict* in your mind about this person.

One such occasion occurred for me when I interviewed a man whose resume stated that he had transferred out of West Point after just two years. His action surprised me, since I knew of the prestige he was giving up by not completing the West Point degree requirements. I said to him, "Your decision to leave West Point puzzles me. I am not sure you are telling me the whole story." It turned out that he wasn't. He admitted to me he was caught in a cheating scandal among the cadets and had been asked to leave.

Don't end the interview with your major concern unresolved—or worse, assume that other people during the day will follow up on your question. Others may not even notice your area of concern, or assume you covered it. To probe a concern before ending the interview, you may have to put the candidate under a bit of stress.

An example of an unresolved concern might be your feeling that a candidate lacks the relevant experience to handle an important part of the job for which he or she is interviewing. In this case, you say something like, "The ability to design questionnaires is an important part of this job, yet I don't see such experience in your resume nor have you mentioned such experience to me thus far. What can you say to reassure me that you can perform this part of the job?"

The president of a rapidly growing high technology company told me he uses stress at least once in an interview to test the candidate for compatibility with his own management style. The method used by the president is to disagree strongly with one specific thing the candidate has said in the interview. For example, if the candidate has explained his philosophy about building a team, the president says: "I would never do it that way. Why would you even bother investing your time with your full staff in that activity?"

The candidate's response to this sudden challenge in the interview is interpreted as evidence of how he might respond in the work environment. If he backs off too quickly, he may be wishy-washy. If he gets hostile or defensive, he'll probably behave in a similar way on the job. The company president uses this specific probe in the later stages of the interview to observe the candidate's response when his thinking is challenged on the spot. The candidate's reaction to this challenge provides insights as to how the individual would fit into the organization's culture and how his management style would mesh with the president's.

Some general managers of advertising agencies use a similar testing device to see how candidates will respond to something stressful they might hear from a tough client. Clients may do this to test the agency's commitment to the ideas they are presenting. It's not unheard of in the agency business to have a client walk into a conference room and, after scanning a wall full of advertising layouts developed by the agency, respond in this way: "This is the worst creative effort I've ever seen. Why don't you take all this trash down and come back on another day when you are better prepared to use my time in a meeting like this?"

To test how a candidate would respond to this situation, a manager could say, "Your portfolio is really pretty awful. Why do you expect me to waste my time on this?" It would be more constructive, and more humane, to pose this as a Situation-Based Question (examples of which are provided in Chapter 12). If a client looked at your layouts and said, 'This is the worst creative effort I've ever seen,' how would you handle that client?"

Another situation where stress is appropriate is when you're interviewing an out-of-town candidate and have some skepticism about whether the candidate would really want to move to accept a job with you. At this point you can say, "I have a feeling that living here would be a big change for you. What can you say that will help me overcome my concern that you'd actually be reluctant to relocate?" This approach puts the responsibility on the *candidate* to reassure you that your concern is not valid.

Placing the burden on the candidate is also effective when your concern arises from "bad vibes" or something unspoken that you have picked up intuitively.

These gut feelings should also be probed: "I get the impression that you are reluctant to take directions from anyone who is less experienced or educated than you are. Has anyone ever pointed this out to you?"

Obviously, you shouldn't start the interview with a stress question: "I noticed on your resume you claimed a dual major in college. I happen to know that's impossible to do at that school." What you "happen to know" may be dated or invalid. As the interview begins, give the person the benefit of the doubt. You can always probe your concern later, without ruining your chance to have an open, relaxed flow of information.

If you wait until the last portion of the interview, you can avoid probing initial concerns that will pass naturally as you learn more about the candidate. But don't introduce your stress question as the *last* one in the interview, or the candidate will leave your office with a negative impression of your company. If you allow interview time after probing your concerns, you can always switch to more conversational topics, like hobbies and leisure-time interests.

The proper use of stress in an interview can help you resolve concerns about candidates and can provide insights into how they might react to certain situations or under certain circumstances. Stress *interviews* are not recommended, and questions that induce stress as a test of the candidate's mettle should be used sparingly and for a specific purpose only.

Another stress-inducer in an interview is *silence*. As an interviewing tool, it can be very powerful, but should be used carefully.

SILENCE AS AN INTERVIEWING TECHNIQUE

Sweaty Palms advises job seekers: "Silence as an interviewing technique is simple. Sometime around the middle of the interview, the interviewer will ask a question requiring a short answer. He gets the short answer. Then he doesn't respond. Nothing. He just sits there, looking at you but saying nothing. What's he doing? You hastily review your answer and retract or qualify it. If you do that, you've made a mistake." If candidates are getting this kind of advice, it is equally important for interviewers to be skilled in the use of silence. Even if the candidate is expecting you to use these techniques, you can maintain control of the interview by using them effectively in the three ways described below.

Most of us are afraid to allow silence to develop during conversations, and that feeling spills over into our interviewing. Yet, when properly used in an interview, the effect it can have on what is said next can improve your interviewing results.

Skilled negotiators know the power of silence when bargaining with others. A lawyer told me after one seminar about a client who was always unnerved by the use of silence in a negotiating session.

He recognized the ploy when it came up, but still had to leave the room to avoid responding to it in a way that could harm his negotiating postion.

Because silence can be so powerful, it is important to understand its most productive use in an interview. Improperly used, silence is threatening to candidates and can leave them more nervous than you want them to be.

People engaged in a conversation feel uncomfortable when a period of silence develops between them. Most of us rush to fill that gap. When this occurs in an interview, remember that the pressure is far greater for the candidate than it should be for you. The candidate can end the silence easily. You shouldn't. Your response to a period of silence in an interview should be the exact opposite of what it would be in a social situation. When you are sharing a meal or an evening out with people, and silence develops, your inclination is to pick up the conversation and keep it moving. You should not assume this role when interviewing. It is up to the candidate to break the silence.

Silence can occur spontaneously in an interview, much as it can in a conversation. However, for silence to be an effective interviewing tool, it should be created deliberately.

When to Use Silence

Increasingly, candidates are being advised about the role of silence in the interview. In *Sweaty Palms*, the author advises: "The proper handling of silence is one of the best exhibitions of power and self-confidence you will ever find in an interview. If you get into a silence situation and use it properly, you can't help but win. Very few interviewees know how to react to silence, and if the interviewer knows what he's doing and you know what you're doing, your feeling of having handled the situation properly will be instantaneous."

To be effective against this kind of advice, interviewers should know about the *three situations* during an interview where the use of silence is acceptable and nonthreatening and can have powerful results.

The *first* time is right after you have asked a Topic-Opener question. Too often, when silence develops at this point, there is a tendency for the interviewer to break the silence and try to qualify or explain the question. Silence at this point is important and should not be disturbed. Candidates who do not respond immediately may be thinking through their answers or considering how much they should tell you. By keeping silent, you give candidates an opportunity to show you some critical skills such as the capacity to organize information, select the most pertinent facts, and respond to an unexpected or difficult question. Being patient with silence can prevent you from jumping in to explain your question ("Well, what I meant was . . .") or trying to answer it yourself. In this way, you avoid telegraphing the answers to your questions.

If the *applicant* is the one letting the silence go on, he or she can easily break the silence by saying, "Would you give me a minute to think about that question?" or by admitting, "I'm not sure I know what you want me to include in my answer."

During this silence, don't stare the candidates down. Instead, communicate in a nonverbal manner that you realize they're thinking through their answer and that they can take all the time that's necessary to organize their thoughts. Some of the nonverbal signals you can give include leaning back in your chair, setting down the pen or pencil you're using to take notes, or looking away from the candidate. Here, your use of silence keeps *you* quiet so you don't answer your own questions.

I also find this technique useful in my consulting work when I am seeking information from employees in a company. When I ask questions, I do not break the silence that follows. Before responding to my questions, some will ask me, "Do you want me to be candid?" or "Do you want a polite answer, or do you really want to know what's going on here?" In the silence before they responded, they have had time to consider whether they really want to open up with me or not.

The *second* way to use silence effectively is after candidates answer questions. When candidates finish talking, a one- or two-second pause before you respond may result in the addition of very rich information to the answer that has just been given. In fact, what candidates say at this point may be more significant than everything else you have heard.

Silence works in this situation because when you pause after hearing an elaborative answer, it's a nonverbal signal that you expect to hear something more. It's almost like saying, "Well, isn't there anything else?"

Another reason this technique works is that silence after a response can be disturbing to candidates' psychological balancing acts. To answer Topic-Opener or other comprehensive questions, candidates probably consider a number of things, pondering whether to share them with you.

For example, if you ask a question such as, "Tell me about your current job," candidates will certainly edit their answers before responding. They will decide what to tell you, what they might possibly tell you, and what they won't tell you at all. If you don't respond immediately to an answer, candidates may go ahead and give you some additional information they had not originally intended to divulge. Your silence encourages this additional disclosure.

The *third* way silence can work for you is as a follow-up to an answer with which you are not comfortable. Consider the following statement from a candidate who has never been west of Ohio until this interview: "I really want to come to Denver when I finish school." This answer tells you nothing about the candidate's motivation and invites a follow-up probe for verification.

One way to employ silence is to repeat the answer without turning it into a question—then remain silent. "You really want to come to Denver." Your silence indicates the answer you just got is inadequate and encourages further elaboration. Silence in this situation is a way to ask "why" without saying "why" or "how come" directly. Repeating the answer and remaining silent is less stressful than probing for more information, and often just as effective.

SUMMARY

Stress and silence are powerful tools that can help you conduct more revealing interviews. It is important to use both techniques properly. Used improperly, stress and silence can be counterproductive to the kind of interviewing recommended in this book. However, their effective use can enhance the overall quality and value of the information you gather in your interviews.

16

You and Your Intuition

*You must spark that feeling in (the interviewer). If you do, you'll probably get an offer. If the interviewer is then asked why he made you an offer, he will most probably reply that you fit the specification for which he was looking. But that's not an accurate answer. Others fit the specification, too, but you hit that feeling and so you got the offer.**

H. Anthony Medley
Sweaty Palms: The Neglected Art of Being Interviewed

You've probably heard people in your organization say, "I had a 'gut feeling' about that guy from the minute he walked in" when referring to a hire that either did or did not work out.

Bob Waterman and Tom Peters, in their book *In Search of Excellence*, suggest that "We reason with our intuitive side just about as much as, and perhaps more than, with our logical side" when it comes to managing and evaluating situations and people.

Intuition can play a key part in an interview, and the weight that you give it in your decision depends largely on how much you believe in it. This chapter gives some pointers on how to recognize the role of intuition in decision making and how to use techniques in this book to verify intuition.

---

*H. Anthony Medley, *Sweaty Palms: The Neglected Art of Being Interviewed* (Berkeley, CA: Ten Speed Press, 1984).

THE ROLE OF INTUITION IN THE INTERVIEW

There are those who believe that, when it comes to interviewing, our minds are set either positively or negatively within a very few minutes after the interview starts—and that the rest of the time is spent verifying our first impression. We form opinions about candidates from the way they dress, walk, talk, sit, and stand—we "read" things into posture, body language, physical appearance, grooming, handshake, and smile. Part of this reaction is based on personal preference or bias, but a major part of it is that feeling or sense that we call intuition.

Webster's New World Dictionary, 2nd College Edition, defines intuition as "the direct knowing or learning of something without the conscious use of reasoning." The key phrase here is "conscious use of reasoning." In fact, when we *intuit* we are *reasoning*, but our subconscious rather than our conscious mind is at work.

When we interview, the gut feeling we get about someone is the result of our subconscious mind weighing the immediate information it is receiving about the candidate against all the things we "know" about ourselves, our company, the people this person would be working with, and our company's culture. Unconsciously, we merge these two batteries of information and draw some conclusions about the candidate's potential for success on the job.

When a candidate comes into your office for an interview, you begin reacting even while you are greeting the candidate, remarking on the weather, offering coffee, pulling up a chair, and putting the candidate at ease. You may be wondering why the person doesn't smile more (or why the smile seems so strained), why the handshake is so limp (or why this person tried to break your hand), why the person doesn't look you in the eye (or why she is staring at you that way). Or you may be thinking, "Wow! This person is really a winner— the perfect candidate for the job!" Your intuition is beginning to work.

Today's well-coached candidates are also sensitive to the non-verbal signals that interviewers pick up on. They tend to play to the interviewer's intuition by the way they dress and by having a polished interviewing style.

156

As the interview continues, our intuition contributes greatly to the bottom-line evaluation of the candidate and, thus, to our hiring recommendation.

The August 1985 issue of *Inc.* magazine contained a story about the founding of Sequent, a successful start-up electronics firm in Oregon. At one point in its early growth, when the company was pressed to meet deadlines, the director of software needed a particular kind of engineer. Although he had found someone that he thought would be competent, one of the other Sequent executives advised against bringing this person into the organization by saying, "You know, it just doesn't feel right." They did not make the hire.

Because intuition is not something that everyone trusts, and because it is difficult to substantiate, many interviewers want to know to what extent they should rely on their intuition when making hiring decisions. How can it be verified? Is it valid?

HOW TO VERIFY YOUR INTUITION ABOUT CANDIDATES

The interviewing techniques used in this book can help you verify—or dispel—your intuitive feelings.

Among the mistakes interviewers make that are cited in Chapter 2 is "telegraphing," or giving candidates clues about the "right" answers. This common mistake has particular significance when you are trying to verify intuitive feelings about candidates. You should say as little as possible about the behavioral expectations of the job and the company culture. Let the candidates reveal their style, their goals, and their expectations so you can measure these qualities against what you know you need and want in the job-holder.

If you intuit during an interview that this particular candidate would not work out, you should try to verify or refute that feeling by asking questions which relate to it. If you sense that the person is too cocky or too independent for your company's work culture or probably does not get along with others, try a self-appraisal question based on an accomplishment the candidate has put on the resume or told you about. "I'm very impressed by the fact that your sales exceeded everyone else's in your department. What, would you say, enabled you to achieve that record?" The person may respond in a way that verifies the cockiness you sense: "I guess you'd say I'm a natural salesman—I hate sales training—I don't have time to listen to all those pep talks and hear other people's boring lectures." This begins to give you hard data which can confirm your intuition, suggesting this person may be difficult to coach and manage!

If, however, the candidate responds that he owes his success to the fact that his fellow salespeople helped him get started, that he wishes the company hadn't made such a big deal of his sales record, and that it was the training and encouragement he received that enabled him to succeed, then your negative intuition might begin to take a back seat. Of course, your intuition might continue to tell you that even though the candidate credits others, he is doing that to just impress you! This is a particular danger if you have already stressed the importance of teamwork in your company.

Be sure you ask enough Self-Appraisal Questions to get a complete picture of the candidate. Intuition, like behavioral premises we form about a candidate's potential for success on the job, may require repeated verification if we are to feel comfortable using it in a hiring decision.

A major danger in interviewing can occur when we intuit before or during the interview that this candidate is *the* person for the job. We can get that feeling when the person walks into the room. We may have it already from reading the resume, or from a recommendation. We say to our co-workers, "I've got a hunch about this person who's coming in this morning to interview for the Seattle job. I think he's the one." If we rely too strongly on our intuition, we may neglect to ask important questions that could reveal critical information about the candidate.

In such situations, interviewers tend to jump to conclusions because they *want* the person to be right for the job. Rather than asking what enabled a candidate to achieve a terrific sales record, we say, "I'll bet you are a real team player and work with others to set and meet sales quotas. Tell me how you managed to achieve such an impressive district sales record." By prefacing a question this way, we reveal not only our intuition about the person (that she'd be great in this job) but also an important clue about what the "right" answers might be. Then, when our intuition is confirmed by a series of "right" answers that we've actually programmed, it may lead us to make a faulty hiring decision. It is therefore just as important to ask probing questions of the person about whom you feel sure as it is to probe for weaknesses in those about whom you have negative feelings.

To the extent that intuition can be verified, questioning techniques that allow plenty of information about the candidate to emerge will help either reinforce or refute the feelings you may have. Self appraisal questions can help verify insights you've gained intuitively from answers to topic opener questions.

HOW VALID IS INTUITION?

The story that follows offers a thoughtful perspective about the validity of intuition.

Scott B. Smith, who edits the *San Jose* (California) *Business Journal*, a widely read weekly newspaper, titled his editorial of June 3, 1985, "Smartest friend I've got: My intuition." The editorial recounts a resignation interview with an employee and Smith's reaction to it— how he was tempted to offer the person more so he would stay, how he began to feel they could not get along without him.

Then, he wrote,

My own experience and intuition finally kicked in. Seemed like eons since I'd had that rush of certainty about such a sticky situation. "You'd better take their offer. In fact, if I were you, I'd get on the phone right now and accept it."

The candidate did, and during the "lame duck" period that followed, Smith began to find out that the person was not everything he had seemed to be. And, over the weeks,

I slowly saw something far more important: I had known all of it. For quite a while, too. I'd known intuitively that his sales were inflated. I'd known his loyalty was fickle. I'd known he'd take any offer that smelled faster, greener. How long had I known? Maybe for months. *Maybe even since before I hired him.* And how had I known? Experience had fed the intuition, of course. The intuition—I call it subconscious intelligence, not at all mysterious—had said the guy was a short-timer, wasn't what we'd hoped, and that I shouldn't have hired him in the first place.

So how come this wonderful intuition hadn't spoken up earlier? How come I'd hired him? Because I'd been hoping for what he portrayed, not what he was in reality. . . . And what, if anything did I learn? Maybe not to describe the job and personality too aptly up front the next time. Maybe not to hire as quickly. Maybe to let my intuition/subconscious speak to me in the middle of the night or whenever.*

Intuition is difficult or impossible to quantify, and it cannot legally be used as justification for not hiring someone. You would have to provide other reasons for not hiring someone if a charge of discrimination were brought. However, this does not mean you should ignore intuitive feelings about a candidate that remain even after you have interviewed thoroughly and talked with others.

SUMMARY

The extent to which intuition figures into a hiring decision depends on the respect that you and others in your organization have for this "subconscious intelligence." In any event, your gut feelings about a candidate shouldn't be ignored. The techniques suggested here can help you verify or counter your intuitive reactions to a candidate.

---

*Scott B. Smith, *San Jose* (California) *Business Journal*, June 3, 1985.

17

Difficult Interview Situations

When questioned, I will give name, rank, service number and date of birth. I will evade answering further questions to the utmost of my ability.

Code of Conduct
United States Armed Forces

So far in this book you have read about a number of techniques that can help you conduct revealing and effective interviews. Most of the interviews you conduct will be under circumstances which can best be described as "normal." Occasionally, however, you may encounter difficulties in interview situations, where you feel you lack some technical expertise or are in over your head. Whether the awkwardness stems from the candidate's behavior, problems in the use of your time, or other challenges, being prepared can help you maintain control of the interview.

FOUR TROUBLESOME TYPES OF CANDIDATE BEHAVIOR

The Unresponsive Candidate (Reticent Ralph)

Saving an interview with an unresponsive or reticent candidate requires a lot of skill and energy on your part. If the unresponsiveness is because the candidate is nervous or guarded, take more time with small talk and use other techniques for creating a relaxed climate. These can include acceptance, compliments, and the playing down of bad news. Sometimes, however, it's not just nervousness: the candidate has something else on his or her mind. If you suspect this is so, you should say to the candidate: "You don't seem to have much to share with me in this interview. Is this a bad day for us to talk, or is there something bothering you that I should know about?"

If the person is troubled by a sudden family illness, accident on the way to the interview, or other circumstance, it may be better to suggest rescheduling your time together for another day.

Unresponsiveness may also characterize someone who is not articulate or who has difficulty answering conceptual questions. You should encourage these candidates to use a conversational approach in their responses. Here is an example: "It sounds as though you are having some difficulty telling me about your current job. Let's imagine this is not an interview and you are merely describing to a friend or relative who doesn't know about your job what you do at work. What would you tell them?"

The Too-Talkative Candidate (Loquacious Lana)

The person who is too talkative presents an equally challenging interview situation. Here, your best defense is a preemptive one. Tell the person at the start of the interview, "I want to learn about you first, then you'll have a chance to ask me some questions." Explain how long the interview will run. "We'll have about 45 minutes together this morning."

If the applicant rambles on and on, remind her you now have less than 45 minutes and you still want to cover several topics. If it's hard to get a word in edgewise, you may have to interrupt: "I'm sorry, although this is interesting, I'm afraid you are giving me too much detail in this area. Can you wrap this up so we can go on to something else before our time is up?"

The Difficult or Hostile Candidate (Angry Albert)

One of the most uncomfortable interview situations occurs when you are faced with a difficult or hostile candidate. This negative behavior, seen in curt answers or sarcasm, may reflect a lack of motivation for the job you have. Or, more specifically, it may be aimed at you. The interviewee may feel that you're not qualified to make the assessment. This more typically happens to personnel people when they must interview someone in a technical discipline. This hostility can occur when the interviewee doesn't know or understand your role in the hiring process.

If the behavior continues to the point where you are becoming uncomfortable or feel you may be losing your objectivity, you should consider asking the candidate directly about what is happening. "I have a task to perform while we are together here in this interview. Yet, I am beginning to pick up some resistance (or hostility) from you that indicates to me that you resent my role in this process. Is there a problem I should be aware of?"

You should avoid getting defensive about your role. If the candidate says, "I'm here for a job in thermodynamics design, and frankly I don't understand the purpose of talking to people outside the area," explain your role. "You'll be talking to several people in that area, but we know it takes a range of skills to succeed in our company. While I won't be probing your technical background, the company would like to know what other skills, interests, and goals you have to help us decide if you are the best person for the job."

The Candidate Who Tries to Control the Interview
(Dominant Don)

Today's candidates are coached in ways to control the interview. One of the techniques a candidate may use is to ask you many questions about the company and the job. This can happen particularly in a screening interview where the person knows little about the open position. Respond to this situation by telling the candidate enough to justify continuing the discussion, but don't give it all away at the beginning of the interview.

Another difficulty arises when it becomes apparent that the candidate's goal is to interview you. Some people may have gotten away with this behavior so frequently that you will have to be unusually assertive to keep the upper hand. If you remembered to establish the guidelines for the interview up front, it will be easier to regain control: "I'll be glad to answer questions about what we are looking for here, after I have a chance to learn about you first."

THE WRONG TIME OR PLACE

Cutting the Interview Short

Some difficult situations involve the use of your time. An awkward situation can occur if, after five or ten minutes, you want to cut the interview short. This should occur only in screening or first-time interviews, when it becomes apparent the person is just not right for the job. It is much tougher to extricate yourself from a long interview if the candidate is in your offices for a full day of interviews with many others as well.

If it is obvious to you that the person will never do, be polite and direct in conveying that it is pointless to continue the interview. There are several vital steps you should follow to minimize damage to the person's ego or to your organization's reputation.

Start by acknowledging something positive about the person or his experience. "You seem to be getting very good experience where you are." Or, "I can see you enjoy what you are doing."

Then say, "However, we have already considered several others for the position who have far more of what we are looking for than you now happen to have. I think it's in the best interest of our time and yours if we cut this interview short." The wording is important here so the candidate believes several others already are far better qualified. Even if he or she is the first one you actually interview, the chances are you have "considered" others.

If you don't take this precaution, the applicant may insist you conduct a longer interview in case no one better comes along.

Predictably, the candidate will want to know what is lacking. Don't be specific. If you say, "We want someone with five years' auditing experience and you have only two," the candidate may try to argue with you: "Yes, but two years where I am is worth five years with anyone else in the business."

The candidate who is way off the specifications for the job may appreciate your candor and actually prefer a short interview to a long drawn-out session where your lack or interest is obvious. Thoughtful interviewers will use some of the remaining scheduled time to give the person helpful advice about other opportunities they may know of or to encourage the candidate to try again in the future.

When You Don't Have Enough Time

When time conspires against you, and you have less than you'd planned on for an interview, you must make the most of it. You may be informed on short notice of a sudden staff meeting, which will cut your planned interview time by two-thirds; or, you may be interviewing a candidate between planes at an airport and one of you arrives late. Whatever the cause of the time constraint, get as much information as you can in the interview time you do have with the candidate.

Acknowledge the obvious: "I'm sorry we won't have much time for the formalities—I want to make the most of the time we have together so I'd like to get right into the interview." In this abbreviated time, have the candiate reveal as much as possible about what motivates him or her. Open with a Topic-Opener question, listen carefully and try to discover what drives the candidate and how his or her mind works.

Follow up with questions that focus on motivation: "Tell me, what has brought you to the point that you might consider changing employers?" or "What do you like about your current job that you hope will also be present in your next one? And what do you want to avoid?"

The reason to focus on the candidate's motivation in the abbreviated interview is that if it's lacking, or not right for your job, you may have enough information to decide that rescheduling a longer interview is not appropriate.

A Noisy Setting for an Interview

Distracting noise can destroy the effectiveness of an interview. Some of the most common—and uncontrollable—noises occur if your office is in an open area or is a partitioned cubicle: you may hear telelphones ringing and conversations in other cubicles. Even if you have an enclosed office, there may be construction going on in your building or outside, or a heated meeting may be going on in the next office or across the hall. It's futile to try to conduct an interview in such a setting. The obvious solution is to go elsewhere. Here are several ideas on alternative locations.

The best choices are an empty office or an unused conference room. However, you may also consider using the cafeteria (if it's not lunch or break time) or even a corner of the lobby. Any of these sites—if they're quiet—are preferable to your office. If none of these is available, consider a nearby coffee shop (not a bar) or even go for a walk around the block with the candidate. You'll get more out of the interview if you take the initiative to overcome the circumstantial barriers. And you may even relax the candidate enough that he presents an unexpected side of himself.

Another device to help you when noise interrupts the flow of the interview is to imagine that a "cone of silence" surrounds you and the candidate while you talk. This phenomenon occurs every day in crowded noisy restaurants where people conduct business over a meal. You can consciously shut out the noise around you and concentrate only on what the candidate is saying.

OTHER CHALLENGING SITUATIONS

The Courtesy Interview

The "courtesy interview" can plague and frustrate interviewers. This type of interview—with someone who is unlikely to be a viable candidate for a current job opening—is conducted as the result of a referral from someone who is important within or to the organization. Courtesy interviews occur at all levels. An employment clerk may be expected to interview the president's nephew. Division heads have confided to me that the president will ask them to consider a "referral" from a major customer or supplier.

To handle this situation smoothly and effectively, you should talk before the interview with the person who has made the referral.

Try to determine the "agenda" of the person who did the referring and the importance of this interview. Discuss with the referring person the criteria for the job and what you look for in a candidate. "As you know, J. D., candidates for our training program should have a college degree, good verbal skills, the ability to work well with others, and a high interest in consumer retailing. Those are the major qualities I will be looking for when I interview Harold." By stating these qualifications at the outset, you will have objective information on which to base your report about the interview. This will also help the referring person, who must ultimately report the results of the interview to the interviewee.

When you conduct the interview, be sure to give the candidate the same courtesy you would give any candidate. Remember that he or she is connected to people who are important to your organization and that his or her impression of the interview will no doubt be shared with others. Show interest, use the interview model to explore a number of subject areas, probe limitations, and remember to end on a positive note.

If there really is no appropriate opening, be sure to convey that information clearly and kindly. "Harold, I've really enjoyed talking with you—your college achievements were impressive. I'm sure that you'll find a training program with an organization that will help you build on that record, and I suspect you'll be an eager and enthusiastic trainee. Unfortunately, I just can't say that we have an appropriate opening for you at this time."

After you interview Harold, provide an itemized response on the candidate to the person who made the referral, beginning with anything positive that you can honestly say. "Here's what I liked about Harold: he has a good degree and seems articulate." Then reveal your concerns. "However, he seems to be a little bit of a loner and I'm concerned he hasn't yet decided what he wants to do." Then provide a wrap-up on what all this means. "In our experience, the best performers in our training program all share a burning interest in retailing. It's too risky to expect this interest to develop after they join us. We find we're better off sticking with those who already know they want retailing. Harold has certain strengths, but first he needs to focus his own career interests. He'll find that once his interests are clarified he can use them as a guide for finding other organizations he can interview with."

The interviewing methods outlined in this book should reveal enough about any candidate that you can deliver a balanced assessment, naming both strengths and weaknesses, even on a referral.

Interviewing Out of Your Discipline or Field

As more companies include peers and subordinates in the selection process, you may face the difficult situation of having to interview someone completely out of your discipline or field. By acknowledging this at the outset you will have a more productive interview. Lead into the interview by saying, "I work in production (or marketing), not engineering, but in our organization we do a great deal of cross-departmental work. Therefore, several of us who are outside of engineering will be talking with you during your interviewing time with us." Then proceed with the interview, assessing those areas that are important to your cross-department work groups (for example, management style, interpersonal skills, interests, and motivation).

Or, if you are from personnel or finance, you might lead in by saying, "You're probably wondering why a nontechnical person is interviewing you for this job! In our organization, we look at much more than just the specific skills and experience needed for an engineering position. We like to have a nontechnical person's assessment as well. Since I'm not an engineer, it will help me if we begin by considering your perception of an engineer's role. What would you say are the most critical skills and abilities someone should have to be a good electrical engineer?" Once you get the candidate to name these skills, ask the candidate to self-assess his or her own strengths against each quality on the list. Ask for examples and third-party assessment of each quality. You will find the techniques covered in this book will serve you well in this situation.

Interviewing "Over Your Head"

Another difficult interview situation arises when you are asked to interview someone who is significantly senior to you in experience and responsibility. Your focus in that interview should be on learning about that person—his or her style, perceptions, and priorities—through a more conversational interview. You will not be assessing performance factors and probing limitations as though you were doing a technical evaluation of the person.

The following is an exaggerated example of an appropriate approach to this kind of interview. Imagine you are waiting off-stage to go on a talk show, and one of the other guests sitting with you is the President of the United States. You could say to him: "You must have a fascinating job. What do you find is the most interesting (challenging, exciting, demanding) part of it?" or "What do you like best about the job?" or "What is one piece of advice you wish you had received from you predecessor before you took office?"

Instead of focusing on your imagined inadequacy in this interviewing situation, think of ways you can draw this person out with just one or two interesting questions.

SUMMARY

Most interview situations will be fairly routine, but from time to time all interviewers will face candidates or circumstances that try their patience and challenge their techniques. The important things to remember are courtesy and control. No matter how difficult the person or the circumstances, be as courteous as possible. No matter what the candidate says or does, stay in control. The techniques given throughout this book will help you skillfully handle even the most difficult interviews.

18

The Decision-Making Process

The shrewd evaluator weighs a man's weaknesses against his strengths to arrive at an overall appraisal . . . he employs a system of checks and balances to determine what asset of the interviewee will compensate for what weakness.

Felix M. Lopez, Jr.
Personnel Interviewing Theory and Practice

When you have conducted one or more successful interviews for an open position in your organization, you should have enough information about each candidate to predict future behavior and begin making a hiring decision. Each step in the interview process has been preparation for this final evaluation. To reach your decision, you will want to review the information you have about each candidate and about the job.

There are three essential components of the interview process that you will want to consider when making your decision: the *candidate/job profile*, your *interview notes*, and the *balance sheet*.

THE CANDIDATE/JOB PROFILE

This is the description you prepared before the interviewing process began (see Chapter 7). It summarizes duties and responsibilities, organizational culture, education, and experience of the Resume Factor and the three Performance Factors: intellectual, interpersonal, and motivational. You may have reviewed the profile before each interview, or this may be the first time you have taken a look at it in a while. In any case, thoroughly critique this profile again. It will serve as a good basis for analyzing the information you have recorded in your notes from each interview and will be compared with information you will record on each balance sheet. As you review those specifications, pay particular attention to the three Performance Factors because of their importance in describing *how* you want the person you hire to handle the job.

INTERVIEW NOTES

Your notes are the second element in the evaluation procedure. Notes are essential to both the process and evaluation of any interview with a candidate. And yet, at least half the people in our seminars resist taking notes during an interview. When the subject comes up, the major reasons they give for *not* taking notes are predictable: it will disrupt the interview, make the candidate nervous, and cause the interviewer to lose eye contact and concentration. These concerns can and should easily be overcome when the reasons *for* taking notes are explained and effective notetaking techniques are explored.

The Importance of Notetaking

Effective interviewing, using the method presented in this book, yields an enormous amount of information. Interviewers who employ these techniques—and use the recommended 80 percent listening rate—will need to record the principal data from the candidate's responses in order to ask self-appraisal questions, make follow-

172

up probes, and develop a pattern of repeated behavioral premises. Notetaking not only supports these essential interviewing skills, it also helps insure that you retain key information about the candidate. Notes from an interview are a key element in the decision-making process.

Only one group of professionals claims their training and livelihood eliminate the need for notetaking. These are litigators—lawyers who argue cases before a judge and jury. They must gather facts, probe witnesses, and retain a vast array of information in the courtroom *without* notetaking.

Unless your own career work has trained you in this same manner, you will benefit greatly from taking notes during an interview.

How to Take Notes

To lower possible candidate resistance to taking notes, first ask permission to do so. No one should object. If someone does, ask why. Chances are you can overcome the objection and put the candidate at ease about the process.

You can turn your request into a compliment. "I would like to learn as much as possible about you, and it's important for me to remember what we talk about. Would you mind if I took a few notes during our interview?"

Jot your notes on a large (letter or legal size) pad of paper. Avoid writing all over the candidate's resume. This practice leads to using the resume as a prop to conduct the interview. Also, you may have the only copy of the candidate's resume. Others will be able to read the resume more objectively if it has not been written on. Using anything other than a large pad of paper leaves little room to write and limits use of your notes during the interview to ask follow-up questions.

Record answers to questions in brief sentences of three to four words. Skip every other line so your notes will be easier to read and evaluate. Because you've followed a model for conducting the interview, a later review of the candidate's answers will remind you of what topic you were covering.

Writing time can be reduced if words are abbreviated, perhaps written without vowels. A candidate's response to the question "What courses did you prefer in high school?" might be recorded as follows: "mth & scnce prefrd." Nearly all the vowels were dropped.

Because the answer to this question evidences an interest area or academic preference, it invites a further probe. Add an underline, star, or checkmark to that note. This serves as a visual reminder to go back and ask a self-appraisal question at an appropriate time rather than cutting off the candidate's answer at that moment.

Hold your notepad upright so that what you are writing can't be read by the candidate. It is surprising how many people can read notes that are upside down. One multilingual banker I worked with told me he switched his notetaking into another language when he observed candidates trying to read his notes. Most people find it easier to hold the notepad at an angle to discourage this.

You should take notes continuously to prevent another mistake in notetaking—the habit of writing down only negatives. If you assure the candidate that the reason you are taking notes is to remember what you talked about, you can undermine an open, relaxed interview if you record only negatives. If you take no notes for the first five to ten minutes, then start writing furiously at the first revelation of some bad news ("I was switched off one account because of conflict with the client"), candidates will infer that you are recording only adverse information.

When taking notes, keep your focus job-related regardless of the topic or time period. You should avoid gratuitous notes that might lead to later legal problems. Notes can actually be subpoenaed if charges of discrimination in interviewing occur. Therefore don't write down words like "newlywed," which could be construed as a code for your suspicion the applicant may get pregnant and leave the job.

A Manhattan law firm recruiting administrator told me of one attorney in her firm who wrote comments about candidates he saw—such as "grew up in Harlem." *Translation*: the attorney doubted that the person's ethnic and social background could contribute to building the firm's practice with affluent clients. This note was unnecessary, illegal, and easily read by the candidate since the attorney also neglected to hold the notepad upright.

How to Use Your Notes During the Interview

Your notes should be used during the interview to ask follow-up questions and probe for accomplishments and limitations. While listening to the candidate and taking notes, you should flag the facts and accomplishments you want to probe. In this way, you will not have to interrupt the interviewee's train of thought. You can go back over your notes and ask follow-up questions when the candidate has finished talking. People are stopped short when you jump in with a question you are worried you will forget to ask. Interrupting is a bad habit some interviewers have. Notetaking during the interview helps prevent interruptions.

Use notes during the interview only to record responses. Interpretation of your notes to confirm behavioral premises is most effective *after the interview*, and is the second step in notetaking. Just as notes assist you in interviewing more effectively, they also help you in your post-interview evaluation of the candidate.

The advantages to taking notes far outweigh the disadvantages. This becomes especially apparent when it is time to make a decision about which candidate to hire.

What to Do with Your Notes After the Interview

If at all possible, go over your notes immediately after the interview. If you are conducting a series of interviews and have limited time between candidates, try to take time during a break or lunch, or at the end of the day, to review them. It's important not to let these notes lose meaning before you interpret them. You may have as many as three or four pages of notes from a 45-minute interview if you use the recommended method of notetaking. To interpret your notes, code every answer that suggests a premise about the candidate's behavior. Use simple codes such as a single letter for each of the four factors; R could stand for Resume (education and experience), I for Intellectual, P for Interpersonal, and M for Motivational. Also record whether or not the factor noted is a strength (+) or a weakness (-). When coding, use a red or green felt-tipped pen so these notations stand out from those taken during the interview. When you have completed this coding, record on a balance sheet the significant behavioral conclusions that came up repeatedly.

The Balance Sheet

In the 1960s, Dr. John Drake applied the recording of applicant qualities to the accountant's balance sheet. Today's version has been condensed to a single-page format, which experience shows busy managers will use. And it is further refined to directly match the factors identified on the candidate/job profile (Chapter 7). This format precludes overemphasis of any one attribute merely because it happens to be listed ahead of others on the balance sheet. It also fosters an objective discussion that can lead to consensus among multiple interviewers.

The balance sheet becomes the third element to consider when making your decision. It is also your principal evaluation tool. The balance sheet requires interviewers to distill the behavioral premises they have drawn about each candidate, and record strengths and limitations against each of the four factors. The balance sheet permits an easy comparison with the candidate/job profile developed before the interview because each is expressed sequentially and in the same terminology against the same criteria.

The balance sheet, excerpts from interviewer notes, and candidate/job profile at the end of this chapter are for a product line manager in an information systems organization. Note how the balance sheet provides an overall assessment of the candidate, how the information it contains is drawn from the notes, and how they link back to the candidate/job profile. This evaluation loop, candidate/job profile-notes-balance sheet, provides an opportunity to make an objective-based decision using predetermined standards for selecting the right candidate for the position.

When the interview process is finished, these records and interpretations provide the basis for your decision.

MAKING THE HIRING DECISION

This process of evaluating candidates starts by comparing the completed balance sheet to the candidate/job profile. Are the most important qualities present in this candidate as strengths? Do

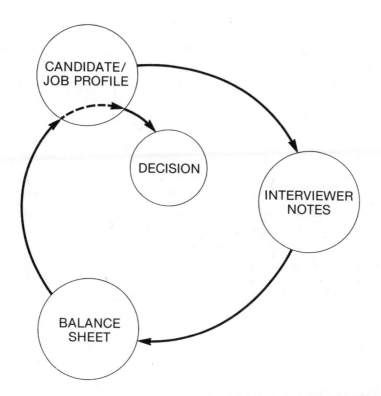

strengths in total outweigh limitations? Are the limitations subject to development or strengthening on the job? If, for example, a candidate for assistant treasurer has never handled foreign currency exchange, can he or she reasonably learn this on the job? Is the candidate a quick learner, highly motivated, competitive? The presence of these performance factors suggests a worthwhile risk that the candidate can learn what's needed on the job to handle foreign currency exchange.

This kind of analysis helps you look at the person's total complement of experience, skills, and potential. It's one of the most useful ways to save an otherwise qualified candidate who happens to fall short on one of the requirements in the Resume Factor. If, for instance, the candidate/job profile lists "five years of financial services marketing experience" and the candidate you prefer has seven years of consumer package goods experience, you need a way to evaluate the candidate's potential for success in this position. Before you reject the person, you should determine the transferability of the marketing knowledge from one field to the other. The candidate will require some special strengths to meet the demands of the job. If the person is conceptual, big-picture oriented, flexible, resourceful, energetic, and willing to learn, you may have identified performance-predicting strengths that will offset the shortcoming in experience.

Compare the balance sheet and candidate/job profile for each candidate you interviewed. You may also want to review your notes again. Recapture the candidate's responses. Remember your reactions. Reevaluate the premises you drew. Respect your intuition. Bring each candidate you are considering back into your mind. Then rank order the candidates according to their fit with the job. Review each of the top-ranked ones carefully against the job profile and against one another. Then you will be ready to make a decision. If none of the candidates measures up, you may have to find more candidates and conduct more interviews.

REACHING CONSENSUS

Most organizational hiring decisions call for multiple interviewer assessments and some degree of consensus. Each interviewer should use the profile/notes/balance sheet process to interpret the interview and evaluate the candidate. Compare the interviewers' balance sheets to see if there is agreement on who is best for the job among all the candidates seen. Where disagreement exists, usually because one interviewer saw the person differently, determine what limitations are getting in the way of consensus. See if the dissenting interviewer can agree that other strengths offset the limitations. Or determine how the others assessed the candidate on those qualities in question. Did they get enough evidence in their interviews to assure the holdout that the risk is justified?

On any factor where there is disagreement, each interviewer should be able to go back to his or her notes and support with evidence from the interview how that factor became a confirmed inference about the candidate.

The balance sheet will lead to more thoughtful, thorough, and consensus-building decisions about the people you hire.

Why Not a Checklist?

When supplying interviewers with tools and forms for evaluating candidates, many organizations think they make the task easier by providing a simple checklist or a way to express an overall assessment for each candidate. The problem with checklists and all-inclusive statements ("Definite Hire" or "No Offer!") is that they offer no real insight about the person and are almost impossible to use to reconcile multiple opinions about the same candidate.

The benefits of this three-component process of decision-making outweigh the extra time it may take to prepare and review its essential elements. Other methods create problems for interviewers and organizations that need to be considered.

Problems with Alternative Methods of Candidate Evaluation

If the job description lists education and experience requirements only, it may be difficult to reject a candidate who meets those standards and yet lacks the motivation or other Performance Factors needed to be successful. All hiring decisions must be substantiated with preestablished criteria for the job in question—otherwise, you may run into legal problems if the candidate feels you can't justify your decision.

Organizations that use all-inclusive or generic statements as their evaluation system may lapse into another decision-making trap: the need to evaluate the evaluator. If Paul says the candidate is "too aggressive," is that in relation to Paul's personality? If so, how aggressive is Paul? Such judgments are subjective and are usually not based on any predetermined list of qualities required for a specific job. They also give the organization little information to weigh.

One small step up the scale from this kind of data about a candidate is the checklist that uses words like "Excellent," "Good," "Average," and "Poor" to rank various attributes. Here is a portion of one such form I found a new client using:

	Rating
Apparent initiative,	__ Outstanding
motivation, intellectual	__ Good
curiosity, alertness,	__ Average
enthusiasm	__ Poor

This checklist lumps together diverse qualities and requires the interviewer to make a one-word judgment about all of them. Further, it provides no frame of reference. Is the candidate "average" compared to what is required in the job, or "average" when compared to others also being considered? Or is the candidate "average" compared to everyone else the interviewer has ever talked to or worked with, or merely "average" compared to the interviewer?

Problems also arise when organizations evaluate candidates by using numerical ratings for many different attributes on a scale from 1 to 10 or 1 to 100.

If one of your employees rated the candidate he just interviewed with a 63 on analytical ability, you probably would ask, "Who gave her a 63?" Such ratings have meaning only when we know who has made the rating.

A major drawback to these forms and checklists is that they usually are not tailored to the specific open job. They are generic. "Poise" may be a highly desirable trait for your head of investor relations but nearly meaningless in assessing a research analyst.

Even a short-form version of a checklist can require 100 judgments about a person (10 traits, each on a scale of 1 to 10). Some call for 200 to 300 judgments. Most busy managers never take the time to do this. Instead, they make just one decision: whether or not they like the person. If they like the candidate, they will clump their checkmarks at the 7–8–9 ratings. If they don't like the candidate, the ratings will be closer to 2–3–4. Some may simply draw a line straight down the page through a single digit—all 9's, for example.

What's happening here is the "halo effect." The person may have been an obvious 9 in enthusiasm, drive, and energy. The interviewer really liked the candidate and had a terrific interview. So she gave him a 9 on everything—from analytical ability to verbal skills.

Sometimes interviewers give uniform rating to candidates they like because they don't want to acknowledge that they have failed to gather information about a particular quality. Interviewers will put down something, knowing full well no one is likely ever to ask them how they arrived at their assessments.

These alternatives may seem like welcome shortcuts in the hiring process, but they don't do justice to the importance of the job you are trying to fill and the value of making the right hiring decision. In fact, they can complicate the decision-making process by failing to provide a total process for evaluating information and inferences about each candidate in a way that will lead to the right decision.

SUMMARY

Making a final decision in the candidate evaluation process requires a thoughtful assessment of the total person and a weighing of strengths and limitations. This process is enhanced when each interviewer has used a candidate/job profile, interviewer notes, and the balance sheet. Samples of each from an actual interview are provided on the next several pages. Using the process recommended in this chapter will lead to more thoughtful, thorough, and con-sensus-building decisions about the people you hire. This process will also help you market the job to the person you decide to hire. Chapter 23, Consultative Selling, will describe this additional use of the balance sheet, particularly as it relates to understanding what motivates the candidate.

INFORMATION SYSTEMS COMPANY

POSITION—Product Line Manager

DUTIES

Bottom-line responsibility for an established product line. Scope includes functional responsibility for product development, marketing, sales, accounting, and operations. Must act upon market opportunities and drive the strategic direction of the organization.

CULTURE

Fast-paced environment of competitive innovation. Position has been open for two months. Will supervise six direct reports; team-building skills are important. Current product requires fine-tuning and some hard decisions.

FACTORS

Resume

– 10 years experience—marketing/operations/planning
– B.S. degree, business
– Management experience

Intellectual

– Analytical
– Decisive
– Strategic thinker

Interpersonal

– Self-confident
– Leader and team builder
– Flexible

Motivational

– Ambitious
– High project-type energy
– Likes a challenge

19

Keeping It Legal

So, if you are among the majority of managers who basically want to do the right thing, and you take a little effort to learn and comply with the various equal opportunity laws, life may not be nearly as complex or frustrating as it is for a manager who chooses to ignore the law.*

Bradford D. Smart
Selection Interviewing

O f increasing concern to interviewers is the growing complexity of laws relating to job discrimination—particularly in the interview process. Interviewers are worried about what questions they can and can't ask, and they're anxious that something they say or do in an interview might be construed as discriminatory.

Their concern is well-founded. Even unintentional discrimination is illegal, and ignorance of the law is not an acceptable defense. Hardly a day goes by but that some job-related discrimination suit is reported in the media—with many such cases decided in favor of the employee. Companies—and the employees who conduct interviews for them—are justifiably interested in "keeping it legal."

---

*Bradford D. Smart, *Selection Interviewing* (New York: John Wiley & Sons, Copyright © 1983). Reprinted by permission of John Wiley & Sons.

To assist companies in this area, there are some specific laws relating to employment discrimination. In addition to understanding these laws as they apply to hiring (they are briefly reviewed in this chapter), there are three important ways you can help ensure the legality of the interviews you conduct.

First, with two simple questions you can test whether an interview question is potentially discriminatory: *Is it job related?* If it *isn't*, don't ask it. *Is it a question* presented only to *a specific kind of person (e.g., a woman or an older person)*? If it *is*, don't ask it, unless you are sure it is permitted for the job situation. For example, based on the job-required tasks, it is legal to ask candidates if they have any physical limitations that would impair their performance on the job. These two tests for any question may seem to oversimplify our complex laws. However, they provide dependable criteria for judging whether a question might get you and your organization into legal problems.

Second, your company should make available to all staff and line employees responsible for interviewing and hiring the current federal and applicable state and local government laws and regulations that relate to the pre-employment process. It's not necessary to read all of the various antidiscrimination laws. However, the pre-employment inquiry guidelines are brief and can easily be reviewed before conducting an interview.

Keep up to date. Remember that these provisions are continually being revised. It's imperative that anyone with interviewing and hiring responsibilities—your recruiters, your supervisors—stay abreast of these changes. Such information is available from the federal Equal Employment Opportunity Commission (EEOC) and the various state and local fair employment practice agencies. Complete details, including full text of official material, can be found in Prentice Hall's *Equal Employment Opportunity Compliance Manual.*

(*Note*: A chart summarizing EEOC's position on pre-employment inquiries appears at the end of this chapter, along with the pre-employment inquiry guidelines issued by the state FEP agency for California.)

As of February 1987, 27 states and the District of Columbia had made published guidelines available. A list of those jurisdictions appears at the end of this chapter.

Third, if you use the interview process recommended in this book, you will lessen the probability of asking illegal questions. Because the candidate/job profile clearly states the qualifications desired for the job, and because information gathered during the interview is linked to that profile for the final evaluation, there is an objective and justifiable basis for the questions you ask and your hiring decision. By asking for examples of past behavior and accomplishments to predict future on-the-job success, you tend to make more objective judgments. When you key your questions to the job specifications, you are more likely to be measuring and evaluating job-related factors.

CURRENT LAWS AFFECTING EMPLOYMENT

The law, as interpreted through the courts and EEOC and FEP decisions, prohibits the use of all pre-employment inquiries which disproportionately screen out groups of people, such as women or minorities, and are not valid predictors of successful job performance or can't be justified as a business necessity. The EEOC and many state and local government FEP agencies publish their guidelines to help employers obey the law during the interview process. The following information provides a brief overview of the key federal antidiscrimination laws. For further information, however, please consult the appropriate agency's regulatory guidelines. Relevant sections of the Federal Uniform Guidelines on Employee Selection Procedures are also reproduced at the end of this chapter.

Note that the state and local government antidiscrimination laws generally parallel the federal provisions or provide *greater* protection to job applicants and employees. Moreover, most state FEP laws apply to private employers with less than 15 employees (the threshold for Title VII coverage, see below); some even cover employers with only one employee. These are the key reasons it is imperative to consult applicable state and local FEP laws and regulations.

Title VII of the Civil Rights Act of 1964

Title VII is the principal federal law protecting job applicants, employees and former employees from unlawful discrimination. It prohibits employers with 15 or more employees for each working day in each of 20 or more calendar weeks in the current or preceding calendar year from discriminating against any individual because of race, color, sex, religion, or national origin.

The Immigration Reform and Control Act of 1986

Under draft Immigration and Naturalization Service Regs detailing employer requirements under the comprehensive Immigration Reform and Control Act of 1986 (published 1-20-87), employers must verify that new hires are legally authorized to work in the U.S. within 24 hours of hiring. These provisions require new hires to produce and employers to inspect official documents, such as U.S. passports, citizenship certificates, alien registration cards, etc., as proof of employment authorization.

The Act's employment authorization requirements for applicant referrals and recordkeeping requirements for employers and others are set out in separate sections and have specific compliance procedures. Beware, however, that the Act's special anti-discrimination provisions prohibit employment discrimination based on citizenship and discrimination against aliens lawfully authorized to work in the U.S. It would, therefore, be wise to check with both the Immigration and Naturalization Service and the appropriate state fair employment practices agency to coordinate your compliance efforts.

Age Discrimination in Employment Act

The Age Discrimination in Employment Act (ADEA) prohibits age-based employment discrimination against persons 40 and older. There is no age cap (with few specific exceptions). ADEA applies to employers with 20 or more employees for each working day in each of 20 or more calendar weeks in the current or preceeding calendar year.

Vocational Rehabilitation Act

Section 503 of the Vocational Rehabilitation Act of 1973 requires employers with federal contracts or subcontracts over $2,500 to take affirmative action for the employment of handicapped people. Section 504 of the Rehabilitation Act prohibits discrimination against handicapped individuals by any employer receiving federal financial assistance. Most states, however, also have laws protecting the job rights of handicapped individuals, and these apply to employers regardless of whether they are government contractors or the recipients of government financial assistance.

Vietnam Era Veterans' Readjustment Assistance Act

Employers with single contracts or subcontracts with the federal government which are $10,000 or more are required by this Act to take affirmative action to employ and advance in employment qualified "special disabled veterans" and veterans of the Vietnam era. "Special disabled veterans" are those who are entitled to compensation under laws administered by the Veterans Administration for a disability rated at 30 percent or more of those persons who were discharged or released from active duty because of a service-connected disability. Vietnam-era veterans are persons who served on active duty for a period of more than 180 days during the Vietnam era (August 5, 1964 to May 7, 1975) and were discharged or released with other than a dishonorable discharge or were released because of a service-connected disability.

Complaint Procedure

Any person who feels that discrimination has occurred, based on any of the aforementioned laws, has a right to file a complaint of discrimination with either the EEOC, the Department of Labor/Office of Federal Contract Compliance Programs (DOL/OFCCP), or the appropriate state or local government FEP agency. The employer must respond to the allegations and articulate a legitimate, non-discriminatory reason for the treatment of the complainant. It is therefore extremely important that all selection criteria used in the selection process be job-related and not screen out individuals because of their race, color, sex, religion, age, national origin, handicap, or veteran status.

WHAT YOU CAN AND CANNOT ASK

The pre-employment inquiry guidelines reproduced at the end of this chapter give examples of the types of questions you can or can't ask in areas of particular concern to interviewers. Your main objective in interviewing an applicant is to determine whether the individual has the potential for performing the job. By focusing on the requirements for the job throughout the interview, you will be able to defend your decisions if a discrimination complaint challenging your selection decision is filed.

Many discrimination charges are based on job interviews. While the majority are settled out of court, many are fully litigated. For example, in *King v. Trans World Airlines (8th Cir., 1984) 738 F. 2d 255*, a federal appeals court ruled that the employer did in fact violate Title VII by asking a female job applicant questions about her plans for pregnancy, childbearing, and child care. This case was ironic because the TWA was in fact able to give three legitimate, non-discriminatory reasons for not hiring the applicant. It lost on appeal solely because the manager who conducted the interview asked the applicant the prohibited questions.

Religious observances, child care, and accommodations of employee disabilities can raise genuine work-related concerns, however. While certain direct questions about these concerns are unlawful, alternative approaches can elicit the information you need.

Work Schedule Conflicts with Religious Observances and Child Care Obligations

Although it is unlawful to inquire about an individual's religion or child care arrangements, questions can be asked of an applicant which will satisfy your need to know about the availability of an individual for work. Prior to asking applicants about their availability for night, weekend, and overtime work and for out-of-town travel, be certain that you understand the specific requirements of the position. For example, *you* should be able to answer such questions as:

● Is this a union-represented position, with shift assignment based on seniority?

- Is night, weekend, or overtime work specifically *required* of the job, or is it *sometimes necessary* to complete the work?

- Is there any flexibility associated with the extra hours; for example, can the employee take work home, work on a Sunday instead of a Saturday, arrange trades with other employees, or come in to work early, as opposed to staying late?

- Are there some similar positions that don't require travel, overtime, weekend, and/or night work?

When you have the answers to these questions, you will be able to interview an applicant and address any concerns that may be expressed about work hours and scheduling. Moreover, if problems concerning religious observances or child care obligations are revealed, you will be justified in probing further into these issues to see if accommodations can be made for the applicants. Here are examples of how to question an applicant to determine if he or she might have problems with the work schedule without improperly raising child care or religious issues:

- "Our sales respresentative positions require frequent overnight travel. Do you have a problem with that?"

- "There are four accounting supervisors, and each must work one Saturday per month in order to supervise the data entry clerks. Will you be able to work one Saturday per month?"

- "We require our paralegals to work overtime and weekends when we are preparing for a trial. Would you be available to work extra hours on short notice?"

- "We have only two warehouse supervisory positions. This means we have to rotate the night and day shifts every eight weeks. Would this arrangement be acceptable to you?"

By phrasing the inquiries with an explanation of the job requirements, you give the applicant a better understanding of the position. Also, the applicant has an opportunity to realize and state during the interview any conflicts that may arise if he or she accepts the position.

If you have some flexibility with the hours of the position, you can determine whether the applicant can be accommodated. For example:

"The position requires weekend work at the close of each quarter. Does this present a problem for you?"

If, for example, the applicant's response is "It will present a problem for Saturday work due to my Sabbath," it would be very helpful if you knew whether or not all of the work could be done on Sundays. You may then inform the applicant that the work can be performed entirely on Sundays, but more work hours would be required. The applicant is then responsible for making a choice based on the information provided during the interview, and may also offer alternative accommodation suggestions for your consideration.

Feasibility of Handicap Accommodations

Knowing specific job requirements is especially necessary when you talk with a physically handicapped applicant. If you are aware of the job requirements, you can present this information to the applicant and, in turn, the applicant can inform you what type of an accommodation may be necessary for him or her to perform the job.

Don't ever assume that an individual can't perform the job-required tasks because of a handicap. Before going into an interview, you should think about the following:

- What are some of the physical requirements of the job (lifting, bending, climbing, confinement to small spaces, reaching, talking, or hearing)?

- What is the physical environment like where the person will be performing the job (is it indoors or outside, subject to extreme temperature changes, hazards, fumes, poor ventilation, noise and vibration, etc.)?

Using the above criteria, the physical requirement of the job can be identified in order to determine an applicant's qualifications. It is essential that these qualifications are verifiable and job-related. For example, a job description should not specify lifting requirement of 100 pounds if the weights actually encountered on the job are always substantially less.

With an understanding of the physical requirements of the job, you will be better prepared as an interviewer to discuss the position with an applicant who has a physical handicap. During the interview, focus on the applicant's capabilities rather than limitations. The following examples demonstrate how an interviewer may address the job-related physical requirements of a position:

- (to an applicant with one arm):

"The position requires climbing a six-foot ladder and placing inventory on the shelves. Do you think you can handle it? Would you need/Would it help if you had any accommodations or accommodative devices? What types?"

or

"The position requires climbing a six-foot ladder and placing inventory on shelves. How would you go about performing this task?"

- (to a blind applicant):

"The assistant engineer must take detailed messages for the senior engineer and prepare work orders. Would you need an accommodation or special equipment to peform these tasks? What type?"

State and local government pre-employment inquiry guidelines—or your own human resources department—may give more examples of how to ask for job-related information without asking questions that can lead to a discrimination charge.

Sexual Orientation

Federal equal employment opportunity laws don't prohibit discrimination based on an individual's sexual orientation. At the state level, only two jurisdictions, the District of Columbia and Wisconsin, provide protection from discrimination on the basis of sexual orientation in their fair employment practice laws. A growing number of local jurisdictions, notable among them are San Francisco and New York City, have laws prohibiting job discrimination based on sexual orientation. Because efforts to urge other jurisdictions to adopt similar prohibitions continue, it is possible that they will amend their fair employment practice requirements accordingly.

AIDS

AIDS (Acquired Immune Deficiency Syndrome) and related conditions have caused employers concern in recent years. At the federal level, enforcement officials appear to be split as to whether AIDS and other contagious diseases are protected handicaps under the federal Rehabilitation Act. The issue is now pending before the U. S. Supreme Court in a case brought by an employee who was stricken with tuberculosis. Most state fair employment practice agencies, however, have indicated that they regard AIDS and related conditions as protected handicaps. The number of AIDS bias in employment complaints being filed and litigated has steadily increased. Most of these cases involve employee terminations or other types of involuntary removals. Employment interviewers should be particularly aware, however, that a growing number of states and local governments (Florida and Wisconsin, for example) are enacting laws that prohibit employers from requiring employees or job applicants to take blood tests that reveal whether they have been exposed to the AIDS virus.

GENERAL GUIDELINES

Above are outlined the principal areas from which a discrimination charge may be triggered, if a job interview isn't properly focused. Other types of questions you should avoid in interviewing are those which inquire directly about a person's race, national origin, native tongue or accent, information about spouse, number and ages of children, date of birth, maiden name of married women, birthplace of applicant and applicant's parents or spouse, and membership in clubs, societies, and lodges other than those relevant to the applicant's ability to perform the job.

The ability to conduct a "legal" interview is increasingly important to employers. If, during an interview, your memory of the federal, state, or local laws should fail, and you're uncertain about whether a question is legal, use the test questions from the beginning of this chapter. (1) Is it job related? (If not, don't ask it.) (2) Is it a question for a specific kind of person? (If yes, don't ask it.)

Subtle Discrimination

While the law is very specific about the more blatant kinds of employment discrimination, another set of more subtle factors can

192

lead to legal problems in an interview. We all have our personal biases, and it's important to keep them out of our interviewing. While the equal employment opportunity laws have made us all more aware of the issue of prejudice, we still tend to stereotype people based on their sex, appearance, level of education, and other such factors. So it's important to keep this in mind.

Remember that prejudgments about people get in the way of the interview. They act as barriers to fair employment decision-making and may also get you, and your employer, into legal trouble. If you don't hire a person, and that person charges that you were biased in your questioning or attitude, you had better be able to document the legitimate, job-related reasons for your decision.

Notetaking

The section on notetaking, Chapter 18, points out the danger of taking "gratuitous" notes. These notes comment about the candidate in a way that can be interpreted as critical and seemingly based on biased inferences rather than facts. Interview notes can be subpoenaed during investigation of discrimination charges. Notes like "Pupils dilated—must be on drugs," or "wheelchair—probably could not travel," or "Vietnam vet—better check references" should *never* be recorded. A good rule of thumb: "Don't write down anything you can't say." If such notes were used in a FEP enforcement hearing, they would cause great embarrassment to your employer and generate bad publicity about your firm—no matter who won the case!

Reference Checks

A key part of the selection process may be reference checking. In Chapter 21, the four principal federal laws which presently and potentially affect the giving of references are reviewed. These laws determine the kind of information you can lawfully ask for and expect to receive from a candidate's previous employers: The Privacy Act (1974), The Fair Credit and Reporting Act (1970), The Family Education Rights and Privacy Act and Buckley Amendment (1974), and the Freedom of Information Act (1966). In practice, they have made many employers reluctant to give information unless it is favorable. The February 1984 issue of *Personnel Journal* carried an article on the consequences of these laws, "Employment References: Do You Know the Law?" The authors conclude that an employer's reluctance to give verbal or written references which contain any negative information makes it more difficult to evaluate a candidate completely. They urge, however, that those giving and those requesting references learn the laws and work within them. The alternative, they conclude, "is a weakened job selection process and letting poor employees move from job to job."

Final Recommendations

Know the laws, particularly for your state, locality, and industry. Keep in mind also that, in limited cases, there may be job-related exceptions to these provisions.

When interviewing, know the job requirements and stick to job-related questions. Be sure candidates understand completely what is required for successful performance on the job.

When rejecting candidates, stick to job-related reasons or simply explain that the person selected was better qualified. Trying to soften the news by telling unsuccessful candidates that they were qualified, but not selected, opens the door for possible discrimination suits.

SUMMARY

Remember, it's not difficult to keep an interview legal, if you follow these basic steps. Review the applicable laws and regulations—essential preparation for any interview. If in doubt about a question, test it in two ways: "Is it job related?" (If not, don't ask it.) "Is it a question for a specific kind of person?" (If it is, don't ask it.) Ignorance of the law is no excuse for conducting a discriminatory interview, and even subtle discriminations as well as obvious bias, can lead to problems with a rejected candidate. Keep it legal.

EEOC GUIDELINES: PRE-EMPLOYMENT INQUIRIES
AND EEO LAW*

When devising or reviewing application forms or seeking information from job applicants, employers should consider two key questions:

- Will using the information to make an employment decision disproportionately screen out minorities, women, or other protected groups?

- Is the information really needed to determine whether the applicant can do the job?

The law, as interpreted by the courts and the EEOC, prohibits the use of pre-employment inquiries and qualifying factors that disproportionately disqualify members of protected groups, if they aren't valid predictors of successful job performance or aren't justified by business necessity (that is, they're necessary to the safe and efficient operation of the business, and no less-discriminatory alternatives are available).

While the laws enforced by EEOC don't explicitly bar pre-employment inquiries concerning race, color, religion, national origin, etc., as do many state fair employment practice laws, it views such inquiries with *extreme* disfavor, since they are usually irrelevant to the applicant's ability to do the job and have traditionally been used to discriminate against persons not protected by the laws.

EEOC assumes that all answers to all questions asked on application forms or in pre-employment interviews are used in the hiring or selection decision. If a discrimination charge is brought, the employer has the difficult burden of proving that the answers were not, in fact, used. It is therefore in the employer's own self-interest to seek only essential, job-related information necessary to determine an applicant's qualifications for employment. The position taken by the courts and the EEOC concerning specific types of pre-employment inquiries are charted on the following pages.

---

*This chart was compiled from a statement issued by the U. S. Equal Employment Opportunity Commission and dated August 1981.

EEOC assumes that all answers to all questions asked on application forms or in pre-employment interviews are used in the hiring or selection decision. If a discrimination charge is brought, the employer has the difficult burden of proving that the answers were not, in fact, used. It is therefore in the employer's own self-interest to seek only essential, job-related information necessary to determine an applicant's qualifications for employment. The position taken by the courts and the EEOC concerning specific types of pre-employment inquiries are charted below.

Subject	Illegal	Legal
Race, Color, Religion, National Origin	All unexplained direct or indirect inquiries may be evidence of bias. State laws may expressly prohibit.	Employers may lawfully collect such information for affirmative action programs, government recordkeeping and reporting requirements, or studies to promote EEO recruiting and testing. Employers must be able to prove these legitimate business purposes and keep this information separate from regular employee records.
Height and Weight	If minorities or women more often disqualified and meeting height or weight limits not necessary for safe job performance.	
Marital Status, Children, Child Care	Non-job related and illegal if used to discriminate against women. Illegal to ask only (or have different policies for) women.	If information is needed for tax, insurance, or Social Security purposes, get it *after* employment.
English Language Skill	If not necessary for job and minorities more often disqualified.	
Education Requirements	If not directly job-related or no business necessity is proven and minorities more often disqualified.	

Subject	Illegal	Legal
Friends or Relatives Working for Employer	Preference for friends or relatives of current workers, if this reduces opportunities for women or minorities. Nepotism policies barring hire of friends or relatives of current workers, if this reduces opportunities for women or men or for minorities.	
Arrest Records	If no subsequent convictions and no proof of business necessity. Mere request for, without consideration of, arrest record is illegal.	
Conviction Records		Only if their number, nature, and recentness are considered in determining applicant's suitability. Inquiries should state that record isn't absolute bar and such factors as age and time of offense, seriousness and nature of violation, and rehabilitation will be taken into account.
Military Service Discharge	Honorable discharge requirement, if minorities more often disqualified. EEOC says employers should not, as matter of policy, reject applicants with less than honorable discharges, and inquiry re: military record should be avoided unless business necessity is shown.	If information is used to determine if further background check is necessary. Inquiries should state that less than honorable discharge isn't absolute bar to employment and other factors will affect final hiring decision.

Subject	Illegal	Legal
Citizenship	If has purpose or effect of discriminating on basis of national origin. *Note*: Questions relating to citizenship must also comply with requirements of the Immigration Reform and Control Act of 1986.	Legal aliens, eligible to work, may be discriminated against in interest of national security or under federal law or presidential order concerning the particular position or premises.
Economic Status	Inquiries re: poor credit rating are unlawful, if no business necessity is shown. Other inquiries re: financial status—bankruptcy, car or home ownership, garnishments—may likewise be illegal because of disparate impact on minorities.	
Availability for Holiday/Weekend Work		If employer can show that questions have no exclusionary effect on employees/applicants who need accommodation for their religious practices, that questions are otherwise justified, and that no alternatives with less exclusionary effect are available.
Data Required for Legitimate Business Purposes		Information on marital status, number and age of children, etc., necessary for insurance, reporting requirements, and other business purposes should be obtained after the person is employed. "Tear-off sheets," preferably anonymous, which are separated from application forms before the applications are processed are also lawful.

STATES WITH PRE-EMPLOYMENT INQUIRY GUIDELINES

Arizona	Missouri
California	Nebraska
Colorado	Nevada
Delaware	New Hampshire
District of Columbia	New Jersey
Hawaii	New York
Idaho	Ohio
Illinois	Rhode Island
Iowa	South Dakota
Kansas	Utah
Maine	Washington
Massachusetts	West Virginia
Michigan	Wisconsin
Minnesota	Wyoming

STATE OF CALIFORNIA
PRE-EMPLOYMENT INQUIRY GUIDELINES

ACCEPTABLE	SUBJECT	UNACCEPTABLE
Name "Have you ever used another name? /or/ "Is any additional information relative to change of name, use of an assumed name, or nickname necessary to enable a check on your work and education record? If yes, please explain."	**NAME**	Maiden name.
Place of residence.	**RESIDENCE**	"Do you own or rent your home?"
Statement that hire is subject to verification that applicant meets legal age requirements. "If hired can you show proof of age?" "Are you over eighteen years of age?" "If under eighteen, can you, after employment, submit a work permit?"	**AGE**	Age. Birthdate. Dates of attendance or completion of elementary or high school. Questions which tend to identify applicants over age 40.
"Can you, after employment, submit verification of your legal right to work in the United States?" /or/ Statement that such proof may be required after employment.	**BIRTHPLACE, CITIZENSHIP**	Birthplace of applicant, applicant's parents, spouse, or other relatives. "Are you a U.S. citizen?" /or/ Citizenship of applicant, applicant's parents, spouse, or other relatives. Requirements that applicant produce naturalization, first papers, or alien card *prior to employment. [Editorial note:* Check requirements of the new Federal Immigration Reform and Control Act of 1986.]

ACCEPTABLE	SUBJECT	UNACCEPTABLE
Languages applicant reads, speaks, or writes.	**NATIONAL ORIGIN**	Questions as to nationality, lineage, ancestry, national origin, descent, or parentage of applicant, applicant's parents, or spouse. "What is your mother tongue?" /or/ Language commonly used by applicant. How applicant acquired ability to read, write, or speak a foreign language.
Name and address of parent or guardian if applicant is a minor. Statement of company policy regarding work assignment of employees who are related.	**SEX, MARITAL STATUS, FAMILY**	Questions which indicate applicant's sex. Questions which indicate applicant's marital status. Number and/or ages of children or dependents. Provisions for child care. Questions regarding pregnancy, child bearing, or birth control. Name or address of relative, spouse, or children of adult applicant. "With whom do you reside?" /or/ "Do you live with your parents?"
	RACE, COLOR	Questions as to applicant's race or color. Questions regarding applicant's complexion or color of skin, eyes, hair.
Statement that photograph may be required after employment.	**PHYSICAL DESCRIPTION, PHOTO-GRAPH**	Questions as to applicant's height and weight. Require applicant to affix a photograph to application. Request applicant, at his or her option, to submit a photograph. Require a photograph after interview but before employment.

ACCEPTABLE	SUBJECT	UNACCEPTABLE
Statement by employer that offer may be made contingent on applicant passing a job-related physical examination. "Do you have any physical condition or handicap which may limit your ability to perform the job applied for? If yes, what can be done to accommodate your limitation?"	**PHYSICAL CONDITION, HANDICAP**	Questions regarding applicant's general medical condition, state of health, or illnesses. Questions regarding receipt of Workers' Compensation. "Do you have any physical disabilities or handicaps?"
Statement by employer of regular days, hours, or shifts to be worked.	**RELIGION**	Questions regarding applicant's religion. Religious days observed /or/ "Does your religion prevent you from working weekends or holidays?"
"Have you ever been convicted of a felony, or within (specified time period) a misdemeanor which resulted in imprisonment?" (Such a question must be accompanied by a statement that a conviction will not necessarily disqualify applicant from the job applied for.)	**ARREST, CRIMINAL RECORD**	Arrest record /or/ "Have you ever been arrested?"
Statement that bonding is a condition of hire.	**BONDING**	Questions regarding refusal or cancellation of bonding.
Questions regarding relevant skills acquired during applicant's U.S. military service.	**MILITARY SERVICE**	General questions regarding military services such as dates, and type of discharge. Questions regarding service in a foreign military.
	ECONOMIC STATUS	Questions regarding applicant's current or past assets, liabilities, or credit rating, including bankruptcy or garnishment.

ACCEPTABLE	SUBJECT	UNACCEPTABLE
"Please list job-related organizations, clubs, professional societies, or other associations to which you belong—you may omit those which indicate your race, religious creed, color, national origin, ancestry, sex, or age."	**ORGANIZA-TIONS, ACTIVITIES**	"List all organizations, clubs, societies, and lodges to which you belong."
"By whom were you referred for a position here?" Names of persons willing to provide professional and/or character references for applicant.	**REFERENCES**	Questions of applicant's former employers or acquaintances which elicit information specifying the applicant's race, color, religious creed, national origin, ancestry, physical handicap, medical condition, marital status, age, or sex.
Name and address of person to be notified in case of accident or emergency.	**NOTICE IN CASE OF EMERGENCY**	Name and address of relative to be notified in case of accident or emergency.

20

Conclusion

The competitive edge in today's economy belongs increasingly to those organizations that select and hire the right people. Effective selection interviewing—long overlooked as a critical management skill—is emerging as a key factor in bringing the right people into organizations.

For many businesses and organizations, these are uneasy economic times. Managers who want to build their organizations, or simply staff their work group, realize skillful hiring of others is one of the few areas in business where exceptional performance can help organizations outpace their competition without spending any more money to do so. This applies to hiring people from within an organization or drawing them from the outside.

The leverage gained by hiring the right people—and the best people—is considerable. Effective interviewing by those making key personnel decisions will have a ripple effect throughout organizations. People tend to hire others who are like themselves. Superior performers that are hired and then trained in these interviewing techniques will recognize and hire other superior performers. Others, who are poorer performers, and poorer interviewers, will tend to hire people like themselves or those who are less qualified and therefore less threatening.

This book has presented proven concepts, strategies and techniques that will give a competitive advantage to managers, supervisors, professionals, and others who make hiring decisions. Set in the context of the demographic and economic issues that characterize the late 1980s, this book should help prepare organizations and individuals for the hiring realities that exist today and that will prevail well into the 1990s.

The scramble for a decreasing number of top jobs will continue as the "baby boom" moves through the workforce, and the trend towards downsizing, mergers and acquisitions will contribute to the further narrowing of opportunities. Well-prepared candidates for jobs at all levels will continue to challenge the skills of those who interview them and put more demand on each person involved in the interviewing process.

Getting Behind the Resume was written to redress the growing imbalance between today's candidates and managers with little or no interviewing training. It seeks to provide strategies that will return the advantage in every interview to the interviewer. By putting control back where it belongs, immediate and longer term advantages are possible for all organizations concerned with maintaining—or gaining—a competitive edge in hiring.

Organizations that already use these techniques have discovered many such advantages. By giving greater confidence to those who conduct interviews, the selection process itself becomes more effective. The perception of the organization by the candidate is enhanced. Fewer costly hiring mistakes are made. Better people are selected. Interviewers learn not only *what* the candidate has done, but *how* the job or accomplishment was carried out. Knowledge of Performance Factors and insights into candidate behavior help optimize the placement of new hires within each organization. Job descriptions that define organizational and job culture as well as desired candidate qualities provide a greater potential for finding the right—and the best—person for the job.

Further, insights acquired about people can be applied to better focus their future on-the-job training and development. This knowledge also helps establish some of the performance standards against which future evaluations can be made.

Exceptional interviewers are not born. Interviewing is a learned skill that can be developed and applied. The benefits of acquiring the skills to conduct a revealing interview far outweigh the investment of time and the practice required. Further, good questioning techniques apply to many other business relationships with co-workers, customers, and suppliers. Exceptional interviewers have a career-long advantage over those who neglect this critical management skill. The principles and techniques presented in this book can play a key role in any manager's preparation for productivity and excellence in hiring and managing others.

SPECIAL SITUATIONS

21

Breaking the Reference Barrier

Another danger is hiring someone who interviews well, but who has performed poorly. Everyone who has ever made a hiring decision knows there are people whose main strength is their interviewing skill.*

Paul W. Barada, President
Paul Barada Associates

Reference checking is a critical step in the hiring process. Because so many of today's candidates are polished interviewers, it is more important than ever to use this step in the final stages of the hiring process.

Reference checking assists interviewers in identifying areas for possible failure on the job that may have been missed in earlier interviewing and evaluations. It is also a way to validate experience and qualifications by talking to others who know and have worked with the person you are about to hire.

In spite of its importance, reference checking is usually the weakest link in the hiring process. Interviewers don't take the time to do it effectively. In far too many cases, they don't do it at all.

---

*Paul W. Barada, *AESC News Report*, Vol. 4, No. 2.

PURPOSE

Reference checking should never be a substitute for thorough interviewing. Instead, it should be a required step in the hiring process—one that follows one or more revealing interviews. It should be done by the person to whom the new employee will report.

The *key purpose* of the reference checking process is to help potential employers *identify any areas for possible failure* missed thus far in the interviewing process. Because the Resume Factor is the factor *least likely* to predict failure on the job, interviewers conducting reference check interviews should focus on whether the candidate's Performance Factors contain causes for possible failure on the job.

Another commonly recognized purpose of a reference check is to verify a job-related track record. The problem with focusing on this purpose is that it tends to lead to verification of the *resume only*—it does not help the interviewer get behind the resume and learn important aspects about the candidate's Performance Factors— the intellectual, interpersonal and motivational qualities he or she will bring to the job.

Because reference checking may seem an overwhelming task, this chapter is designed to explain it fully and to give you several methods for doing it. The short-form version uses a more conversational approach and provides an easier way to get started and to build your self-confidence in this skill.

VALUE OF REFERENCE CHECKING

At a major New York bank, a key executive with excellent credentials, recruited from the Midwest, resigned after five months. The reason? His family was unwilling and unable to make the transition from the Midwest to New York.

At a West Coast-based international computer company, a marketing executive with an impressive career history was ardently recruited and then let go after less than three months. The reason?

She didn't catch on quickly to the way things had to be done in that company's culture.

At a Midwestern advertising agency, a highly sought-after creative director was recruited from New York and let go within a year. The reason? Although his creative work was exceptional, his arrogance prevented him from working effectively with the people he needed to associate with on the job.

In each of these cases, careful reference checking might have prevented a costly mistake for the company—and the individual. Consistent in each example is the fact that someone with sound credentials and an excellent job history was sought out by a company and yet failed on the job. Such stories are not uncommon, and they point out the importance and value of doing thorough reference checking as a follow-up to conducting revealing interviews with candidates.

The value of conducting reference checks in a way that gathers information that will help predict success or failure on the job should not be overwhelmed by actual and perceived barriers to gaining such information.

PERCEIVED AND ACTUAL BARRIERS

There are a number of obstacles to reference checking that most experienced interviewers have confronted. These barriers underscore the need for a sound strategy and thorough preparation for this kind of interview.

Legal Barriers

The most serious barriers are legal ones stemming from laws passed in the '60s and '70s to protect equality and privacy and to insure equal employment opportunity. Potential references are reluctant to talk freely because of the reporting requirements these laws contain and the possibility of potential lawsuits based on defamation, negligence, or intentional infliction of emotional harm. Laws protecting employees against discrimination in hiring can also apply to statements from previous employers. These statutes, discussed in Chapter 19, "Keeping it Legal," include Title VII of the Civil Rights Act of 1964 (as amended), the Age Discrimination in Employment Act (ADEA), the Rehabilitation Act (1973), and the Vietnam Era Veterans Readjustment Assistance Act (1972).

Here are key points in the other federal laws that affect reference checking in particular:

The Privacy Act (1974) allows individuals to bring suit for damages if information in records maintained about them is used for a purpose other than that for which it was collected.

The Fair Credit and Reporting Act (1970) protects individuals in terms of any investigative credit report to the extent that the individual being investigated has the right of access to the information obtained. Information relating to character, reputation, or personal characteristics may come up when the background of a prospective employee is being investigated. If this information is obtained through "personal interviews with friends, neighbors, or associates," then special notice must be given to the individual by the one providing the information.

It is easy to understand why would-be references would just as soon say nothing.

The Family Education Rights and Privacy Act (Buckley Amendment) of 1974 affects companies obtaining certain information about a student without prior consent.

The Freedom of Information Act (1966) makes information held by agencies of the federal government accessible to individuals in the private sector.

In addition to these laws, common law affects references if a question of defamation arises when communication about an individual is judged false and harmful to his or her reputation. (Libel is defamation by writing; slander is defamation through speech.)

Other Barriers

The amount of time required to effectively check references is a generally unrecognized barrier. Ideally, several references should be obtained from each of three organizational levels: the candidate's superiors, peers, and subordinates. But getting even one reference from each level entails a total of three interviews—which requires more time and effort than the candidate interview itself!

The time constraint is exacerbated when no thought is given to checking references until the job offer is made. At that point, momentum is focused on landing the candidate and filling the position. Little incentive remains to raise fresh doubts and to act on them.

Lack of candor from references is yet another formidable barrier. When references are called, full disclosure is often difficult to obtain. Establishing rapport with a stranger over the telephone is challenging under the best of circumstances, and what makes matters worse is that the whole area of reference checking is uncomfortable for many people.

Add to this difficulty the fact that many organizations warn their employees not to respond to such inquiries. Instead, they are told to refer questions to the Personnel Department, which in turn is instructed only to confirm dates of previous employment.

Finally, the person checking references must guard against bias, which can enter the picture in three ways: (1) only friendly referrals picked by the candidate are contacted; (2) a particular source is biased; (3) an individual referral's perspective is limited.

The balance of this chapter focuses on ways to overcome these barriers and do effective reference checking.

OVERCOMING LEGAL BARRIERS

One recommended way to overcome the legal constraints is to obtain a written release from the prospective employee to conduct reference checks.

Getting such permission may be easier for managers than they think. A simple way is to include it on the application form, especially if all candidates are asked to fill out and sign one.

Included in this form can be a statement of approval to check on references. Here's an example:

> I understand that an investigation will be made of my past work history and my personal character, which investigation must be satisfactory in order for me to continue in the employ of the Company, and that any falsification of fact in my application will result in immediate discharge, regardless of when discovered.

If your present form lacks such an agreement, consider revising it. Exact wording should be cleared with an attorney.

>>>**GET CLEARANCE** → Your reference check shouldn't jeopardize a candidate's current job. Contact a current employer only with the candidate's prior approval and only if you're seriously considering making a job offer. You may wish to condition the employment offer on the present employer's having confirmed compensation and other claims made by the candidate.

When you call a reference, assure that person that anything said will be kept confidential. If you have a release from the candidate, tell a reluctant reference: "I am authorized by the candidate to contact you." Be careful, however, about saying you have a "written release." This may alarm the reference and then be counterproductive to getting a response. You should keep detailed notes on what you learn and write up your findings with generalized quotes, not ones directly attributed to a specific source. Write that "A previous supervisor commented, '. . . ,'" not that "Elizabeth Blackmore, his former supervisor, said '. . .'"

WHAT TO EXPLORE IN A REFERENCE CHECK

There are at least 10 areas you can probe in a reference check to help confirm or expand what you already know about the candidate and reveal any issues missed to date that may lead to failure.

1. Management style.

2. Strengths and weaknesses (e.g., technical competency, management style, political savvy).

3. Perceptions of others in reporting relationships with the candidate—superiors, peers, and subordinates. These come from

insiders and can include dotted-line or cross-department relationships.

4. Perceptions of outsiders (such as consultants and vendors).

5. Insights on personal character, lifestyle and relocation issues, etc.

6. Verification of information furnished by the prospective candidate in the resume and personal interview (for example achievements, compensation components, reasons given for departure from previous or most recent employer).

7. Perceived vs. actual role definition and performance/contribution.

8. The candidate's ability to perform vis-a-vis the employer's position specifications, goals, and other factors such as the size of the organization and management structure (centralized vs. decentralized, line vs. staff).

9. Prospective candidate's fit with your culture.

10. Prospective candidate's career potential.

HOW TO CHECK REFERENCES

Effective candidate interviewing will limit the scope of what needs to be covered in subsequent reference checks.

The following two formats are suggested for conducting a reference-check interview. The long form ensures you will cover all the major topics and increases the likelihood of discovering any undetected causes of possible failure if the candidate is hired. The short form is only for verifying the job-related track record and then probing any specific concerns you have from your own interviewing of the candidate.

If you do a thorough job of getting behind the resume and understanding the candidate, the short-form reference check may be all you need. The short form can be looked upon as a reward for doing thorough interviewing in the first place.

LONG-FORM REFERENCE CHECK

Suggested questions are arranged under major topic headings. As you confirm data under one topic, you may be able to limit its coverage when calling subsequent references. The first two topics and the last are also used in the short form.

Qualifying the Reference

☐ How long have you known the candidate? In what context?

☐ State your own understanding of the candidate's title and role and ask the reference to confirm that understanding.

Confirming Job Data

☐ How long was the candidate's tenure with the company and in each role or title?

☐ To whom did the candidate report? What was the nature of their working relationship? Who reported to the candidate?

☐ Describe the candidate's job responsibilities, product line, size of budget, sales volume, client list, etc.

☐ What was the candidate's compensation—salary and bonus?

Working Relationships

☐ How did the candidate get along with superiors, peers, and subordinates?

☐ What was the most effective way to communicate with the candidate? (Directly and to the point? With persuasion? Logically rather than emotionally?)

☐ What motivates the candidate?

Management Style

☐ Describe the candidate's management style and how he or she altered it for different people or situations.

☐ Describe the candidate's approach to and results from training, developing, and promoting subordinates.

Accomplishments

☐ What were key achievements in his or her tenure in each role?

☐ What else could the candidate have done to improve upon those results?

☐ Here are some accomplishments from his or her current resume. (Read them.) Could you comment on their accuracy?

Product Knowledge

☐ What was the extent of the applicant's product knowledge?

☐ How would it be described by others—vendors, customers, dotted-line reports?

Behavioral Qualities and Strengths

☐ List some adjectives to describe the candidate's management style and specific behavioral qualities (for example, decisive, participative, authoritative, politically savvy, aloof). Ask the reference to pick the most appropriate ones.

Potential

☐ What was the candidate's career path and future within the company (was he or she on the fast track)?

☐ What is his or her growth potential? How far can this person go?

☐ What role would best suit the candidate? Describe your most realistic career-plan scenario for the person (his or her next job or ideal work environment, for example).

☐ What is needed to insure this person's future growth and development?

☐ Why did this candidate leave the reference's organization? If it was "for more money," why didn't he or she get it there?

☐ Review the position description with the reference and ask his or her appraisal of the candidate's fit with the description.

Closing

☐ What else can you tell me that will help round out this picture of the candidate?

☐ Whom else should we contact as a reference? Who would be the candidate's critics?

SHORT-FORM REFERENCE CHECK

From the long form, cover these three topics: Qualifying the Reference, Confirming Job Data, and Closing.

An illustration of the short form reference-check interview follows the section on contacting references.

CONTACTING THE REFERENCE

The ideal conditions for conducting a reference-check interview occur when you know the reference personally. When that happens, you are apt to receive more candid and useful information.

Unfortunately, we don't live in an ideal world. It's more likely that you'll have to call a stranger and try to talk that person into taking a seemingly big legal risk to tell you anything at all about a former employee or colleague. The reference not only doesn't know you, he or she may have no incentive to help a total stranger and may resent taking the time to talk to you. Because reference checking is so integral to the hiring process, you'll have to find ways to overcome these potential detractors. One way is to learn something from the candidate about the previous supervisors. This can be useful in building rapport when you call that person for a reference.

The first step towards conducting a successful reference check interview is adequate preparation. After your interview with the candidate, identify areas of concern you wish to corroborate or gain more knowledge of. List those areas, with specific questions. Also, have a copy of the candidate/job profile, so you can share this information to help the reference speculate as to how well the candidate will match the job and fit with your culture.

When you call, ask "Is this a good time to talk?" and acknowledge that the interview could take as long as 15-20 minutes or more. If the reference can't speak with you at the time you call, ask when it would be convenient for the two of you to talk.

Your goal in this interview with the reference should be to win that person over to the idea that the two of you can be partners in helping the candidate make the right career choice.

If it's a critical position you are filling, you might even consider offering to personally visit the person giving the reference. If the reference wants to know why you are doing this, suggest that this is a private matter and you'd like to give it the proper attention.

USING THE SHORT FORM TO CONDUCT A REFERENCE-CHECK INTERVIEW

To open the interview, identify yourself and explain you are helping someone the reference knows to take the next career step. Name the candidate; in this illustration, it's Harry Wilson.

Explain that you are considering Harry for a position in your company and this represents a big decision for both parties. The reason you are calling is to help insure that this is the right job for Harry and that you would not be setting up a possible failure for him.

Throughout this interview, you should be emphasizing the consideration of what is best for both parties rather than conducting an inquisition to discover what's wrong with the candidate.

After you qualify the reference and confirm job data (the first steps in the Long-Form Reference Check), get the reference to talk in general terms about the candidate: his previous job, what he did, how he did it, and the like.

Using a Topic Opener is appropriate here. Then sit back and listen. You must allow the necessary time for all the good things about the candidate to come out. This helps to relax the reference and reinforce the sense that he or she is doing well for Harry.

Once the reference stops talking, you can ask for more. "What else can you tell me about Harry?" When the reference appears to have said all he or she is going to at this time, offer your thanks for being so helpful. Then ask if you can follow up on several things that were mentioned. Here is where you should begin to use the specific questions and probes you have developed to round out and confirm the information you obtained during your interview with the candidate. This is no time for general questions (such as, "Is Harry a good manager?") that are likely to yield vague answers. Also avoid questions that telegraph an answer: "Is Harry pretty honest?" or "Can Harry handle negotiations?"

If Harry's skills in motivating others are a question mark for you, that is an area for you to probe. Lead into this by mentioning something the reference has already disclosed. "You mentioned that Harry supervised three other people in your department. Could you tell me a little about his skills in motivating subordinates?"

As you listen to each answer, be sensitive to the reference's enthusiasm and conviction. Is he or she really "damning the candidate with faint praise?" Also be sensitive to voice inflection, the choice of words, and any hesitation in answering a question.

To determine the evaluative criteria of the reference, ask the reference to rate the candidate on a scale of 1 to 10 in terms of overall effectiveness as a motivator. Or ask how he rates in this skill compared with other employees in similar positions. Ask how others in the organization might assess the candidate on the same scale.

If you suspect an answer is glossing over the truth, acknowledge your surprise. "It sounds as though you see Harry as a good motivator. Can you give me some examples of the effective ways that Harry motivated others when he was working for you?"

Once you have probed about specific skill areas, you can then inquire about other unidentified needs. "As you think back on Harry's performance for you, what would be the one thing you would like to see him improve on to make the most of this new opportunity?" Or, "We have a strong commitment to professional development in our organization. What would be the first thing we might do for Harry to help him grow professionally?"

Then you can ask the reference to give you some thoughts and comments about roles in which Harry seems to function best.

As a wrap-up for the interview, tell the reference about the culture and work environment in your company. Ask the reference to tell you how well he or she thinks Harry will fit in and how relevant his previous work is to this new situation.

Thank the reference for the help that has been given and restate how important this upcoming decision is for both your company and Harry. Tell the reference you will probably be deciding within the coming week about next steps. Then provide your office and home phone numbers in case anything else comes to the reference's mind that would add to what already has been said. (This provides a face-saving way for references to come back several days later about something on which they haven't been totally candid.)

HANDLING PROBLEMS

When calling for a reference, if you are told: "It's against our company policy to provide references" ask, "Can you verify the title? dates of employment? salary?" Then say, "Your answer to a few other questions would be quite helpful." In other words, get what you can, then push for more.

If the reference you contact isn't opening up, consider providing some "for instance" adjectives (authoritative, calm under pressure, motivates others, etc.) to which the reference can respond. Ask for examples to support the adjectives the reference has chosen.

If you are having difficulty finding out about the candidate's limitations, point out to the reference that everyone has shortcomings and you want to make sure this opportunity is well suited to the candidate's blend of strengths and limitations.

If you get evasive or non-answers, probe for specifics. "Harry is very decisive." Ask about the quality of his decisions or how much acceptance he got for them. Use a self-appraisal question to probe for more detail. "You said Harry is a good manager; what is it about him as a manager that makes you say he is good at it?"

If you run into negative disclosures about the candidate, probe for a factual basis for these statements. Ask the reference to explain what happened. Ask if the problem was due to unfortunate politics, a changing of the guard, or a personality clash. Ask for another reference with whom you can talk about this, perhaps someone who was employed in the same department at the same time. Check the negative reference with other sources before using a single disclosure to make a decision about a candidate. Be sure to "reference the reference" source when you get a negative disclosure about the candidate.

To avoid getting only friendly referrals picked by the candidate, ask each reference if they can refer you to someone else who also could comment on Harry's work. Finally, when you do get reference names from the candidate make sure you ask for supervisors, otherwise you may just get the candidate's friends and co-workers who lack perspective.

SUMMARY

Reference-checking interviews are extremely challenging yet enormously important in evaluating today's candidates. Such interviews require you to be aware of protective laws while attempting to gather information from individuals who may be reluctant to cooperate. Thorough, in-depth candidate interviewing minimizes your dependency on reference checking. The success of reference-checking interviews can be enhanced, however, by advance preparation and the application of many of the skills presented in this book.

22

On-Campus Interviews

A screening interviewer is looking for a reason to reject you rather than a reason to accept you. Don't volunteer anything in a screening interview.*

H. Anthony Medley
Sweaty Palms: The Neglected Art of Being Interviewed

I t is a paradox that on-campus interviews—the most important interviews for bringing new talent into an organization—are the shortest and most exhausting to conduct.

Compounding this problem is the fact that many schools are providing superb counseling advice, even videotaped practice interviews, to prepare graduates for any challenge they may encounter. Further, college bookstores sell many volumes of advice to students. The book quoted at the start of this chapter, *Sweaty Palms: The Neglected Art of Being Interviewed,* is one of the best-selling books on campus.

---

*H. Anthony Medley, *Sweaty Palms: The Neglected Art of Being Interviewed* (Berkeley, CA: Ten Speed Press, 1984).

To make the most of this demanding form of interview, it's important to understand its purpose. As with all other interviews, it's also important to be well-prepared, conduct the interview effectively, take useful notes, make the right decision, and use proper follow-up techniques with everyone you interview.

This chapter provides advice on conducting the on-campus interview and attracting those you want for a second visit. Related activities of college relations—selecting schools, contacting the placement office, scheduling recruiting dates, and providing recruiting materials—are beyond the scope of this discussion.

The purpose of on-campus interviews is to screen a large list of candidates and to select a group to be called back to your company or offices for further interviews. You should invite back only those students you're highly confident will receive an offer.

The key assessment you must make is "Overall, can this person work effectively in our company and grow with the job?"

On-campus interviewers should avoid inviting back borderline candidates. Sometimes interviewers will say, "Well, I didn't particularly like her, but based on her academic record I felt others should see the person and decide if they liked her better than I did." On-campus interviewers should have sufficient experience and wisdom to make good decisions after these brief meetings with many students.

As a rule of thumb, expect 20 to 50 percent of the candidates you see to be worthy of a call-back invitation.

If you're not hitting even the minimum percentage (three call-back invitations out of a schedule of 15 students), one of the following may be the reason:

1. You're recruiting at the wrong school.

2. You're not seeing enough of the best students on campus.

3. Your recruiters' standards are unreasonable.

Something may be wrong with your college relations and pre-recruiting activity.

PREPARATION

Before the First Interview

On arrival, register at the Placement Office about one-half hour in advance of the scheduled time for interviews. (Get there an hour early if you haven't yet received resumes of those on your schedule.) Then do the following:

- Identify the room or cubicle assigned for the interviews and the method of identifying the next student on the schedule.
- Determine the number of students on your schedule and the time limit for each interview.
- Confirm the luncheon arrangements made for recruiters.
- Get out notepaper, a pencil, and a wristwatch so as to stay firmly on schedule. (Students' class schedules or other interview appointments allow no leeway.)
- Prepare a summary list of everyone you will see by time of interview. You will mark special notes on this list and use it to determine your flexibility to make any schedule changes during the day.

Resume Review

Review all the resumes of students on your schedule. Next, divide the entire group into two subgroups. The first group consists of resumes of those you expect will receive a call-back after you interview them. For this group, decide how to probe the interpersonal and motivational factors in the interview. You already know these candidates have a strong Resume Factor, so you'll want to focus on what kind of people they are and what motivates them. Assessing the interpersonal factor is important for determining the candidate's fit with your organization, and determining the motivation factor will give you insight into how to sell them on a call-back interview and perhaps a job offer.

With the second group of resumes, look for experience areas you might explore to to uncover a "diamond in the rough." This process will help you conduct more productive and open interviews with all students on your schedule.

CONDUCTING THE INTERVIEW

Typically, you have just 30 minutes for an on-campus interview. At most law schools, only 20 minutes are allowed for each interview. It therefore is not uncommon to see 12-14 students in a single day, and perhaps as many as 24. Since each interview comes one right right after the other, it is an exhausting and challenging day. To conduct effective and revealing interviews under these circumstances requires application of many techniques covered earlier in this book.

Opening the Interview

Open each interview, after greetings and introductions, with a statement like the following: "I've already reviewed your resume, and during our short time together I'd like to learn more about you. I'm going to ask you some questions during the first part of the interview. Then I'll give you a chance to ask me questions about our company." This lets the candidate know how you expect the interview to flow. You should use about 70 percent of your time together for assessment purposes.

Questions

You will have time for two or three Topic-Opener Questions. Resist the temptation to open each interview with an identical question, "Tell me about your years here at Northwestern." Instead, use a variety of Topic Openers that will keep you, and the students you interview, from being needlessly bored. Given the limited amount of time, you may want to narrow the Topic Opener slightly to get immediately at information of interest to you. Here are four topics, all relevant for opening this interview. "Let's start by having you talk about. . .

". . .your high school years (college years, if it's a graduate student) and your decision to come here to Northwestern."

". . .your part-time and summer jobs while you've been enrolled in school and what you've learned from them."

". . .your interest in a career and what the ideal first job for you would be."

". . .your assessment of your education to date, the ways it has benefited you, and what you'd now change as you look back on it."

If any of these questions lead quickly to a question about your company, remind the student you want to learn about him or her first, and that there will be a chance to ask questions at the end.

The initial response to your Topic-Opener question may be a short reply. If it is, try a few seconds of silence to signal you expect to hear more. If this doesn't work, probe further. "What else can you tell me about that?"

You should get some reading on the motivation factor for every student you see on campus. Because students compare notes with one another after their interviews, be sure to rotate your questions. If you develop a dozen questions to measure motivation, you can ask each interviewee two of them and not have to repeat any question until you have interviewed six students. These questions should be written on 3″ by 5″ cards before the interviews begin. Here are a half-dozen sample questions for probing the motivation factor. Note that each is open-ended, beginning with "what" or "how."

1. What long-term satisfaction do you expect to derive from your career?

2. How do you evaluate your college years as preparation for your future career?

3. What are your thoughts about this line of work in an organization that would sustain your interest and motivation in the years ahead?

4. How do you select which companies to sign up with for interviews?

5. What would be some of your concerns about any company?

6. What made you decide to sign up with us?

On-campus interviewers should also have standard answers to questions students ask frequently. Subjects that come up include methods and timing for performance review or salary adjustments, maternity leave policy, interoffice transfers, insurance benefits, vacations, etc. A prepared list of brief answers helps to reduce the interviewer's fatigue and eliminates the likelihood of a student hearing a different answer to any question on a call-back visit to your company.

It is best not to probe for limitations in an on-campus interview. The nature of the interview provides enough stress on candidates, and you will want to use the little time you have to relax them and get them to open up .

Notetaking

There should be no question in your mind about the necessity for taking notes when interviewing on campus. Individual students will be blurs in your mind long before the day is over if you don't take notes.

Further, many interviewers overlook the fact that most students are concerned if you don't take notes. There are two reasons for this. First, they know you will be seeing students in back-to-back interviews all day. Students are concerned you won't be able to remember them specifically if they don't see you taking notes. Second, some students may assume the absence of notetaking by the interviewer means they have already been rejected simply on the basis of their resumes.

Take notes following suggestions provided in Chapter 18. Because on-campus interview facilities tend to be small and cramped, it's especially important to hold your note pad upright so the student can't read your notes. One alternative to this was suggested to me by an attorney who interviews at several law schools. He says he takes a minute between interviews to dictate notes and impressions into a pocket dictating machine. He describes this as "dumping memory core." That phrase graphically describes what you must do when conducting back-to-back interviews. Gather as much as you can to assess each student individually, then *clear your mind* before the next interview.

Part of your notetaking during the day involves an unusual but very useful step. After *every* interview, force yourself to make a preliminary judgment regarding a call-back invitation: yes, no, or maybe. Then, during break and lunch times and again at the end of the day, continually review and revise your evaluations. This will be tough to do for the first few interviews, because you don't have a feel for the total schedule and the caliber of students. This discipline, however, will allow you to sort through a large number of interviews in a single day.

Closing the Interview

Once you have completed the evaluative phase of the interview, you should have about 30 percent of the time remaining. You should conclude with a wrap-up question to make certain you've learned what you should about each student. Use questions like these: "Is there anything we haven't covered that you feel I should know about?" or "What more would you like me to know about you before I answer your questions?"

This is the time when you answer questions from the students and do whatever selling is necessary to get the most promising students to come to your company for a second interview. Remember that the purpose of the on-campus interview is to select for call-backs students you are highly confident will receive an offer. Selling is *not* the major purpose of this interview. It should occur only in the latter stages of the interview, after you've assessed the student.

Even those you intend to call back shouldn't be told so at the time of the interview. You should close interviews uniformly, by telling each student that within two or three weeks you or someone from your company will be in touch regarding the next steps. There are several reasons for avoiding a commitment to a call back at the time of the interview.

● The "star" you see at 10 a.m. may pale in comparison with others you see later.

● It puts you in a difficult position with students you do not intend to invite for a call-back interview. If their friends have already been invited, then you can't honestly say, "After we return to our offices we review our interviews with every student before deciding whom to call back."

● When you review your interview notes back at the office, you may decide to invite students in addition to or other than those you had originally selected. If you have already extended invitations, the students you invite after the interview day may feel like second choices. And you may have second thoughts about some you originally thought were likely candidates.

MAKING YOUR DECISIONS

In a full day of interviewing, you will see a dozen or more students. From these, you will want to select a few to invite for further interviewing. Try to make your decisions as quickly as possible after you see the last students. Otherwise, your impressions may become hazy and it will be difficult to make your selections.

Compare your notes from every interview with the preliminary judgments you made after seeing each student. This is not a full assessment interview, so you will not be completing a balance sheet on each student. Instead, you will develop three lists of names for call-back invitations: yes, no, and maybe.

After you develop these lists, rank order all the "yes" decisions and pick the first one or two runners-up from among the "maybes." Be sensitive to the time-of-day phenomenon that can impair your judgment: By midafternoon you're tired and perhaps bored. So are some students who have been interviewing with other companies as well. Since you and the student you see at 3 p.m. are both fatigued, you may decide he or she isn't as good as the one you saw at 9 a.m. Review your evaluation of each candidate relative to the time of day you conducted the interview.

The temptation to invite back marginal or borderline candidates is greatest when conducting interviews at schools that are nearby or those with many alumni already working in your organization.

At nearby schools, the rationale often heard is "Well, it only involves a small travel cost." Unfortunately, there are other costs as well. First, the time of many of your own people is consumed during a busy recruiting season. This can deplete the energy and enthusiasm of your most effective in-company interviewers. Second, your company's image on a particular campus can be damaged if really top students begin to question your selection standards. Students know what their classmates have to offer, and some highly desirable candidates may pass up your invitation because they feel they would not be in a select company.

Restraint must also be exercised when selecting call-backs from a school with many alumni already employed by your organization. No matter how successful your current employees from this school have been—and how much they would like to see more of their fellow alumni get hired—you should resist inviting back marginal candidates from these schools, too.

When you have confirmed your list of "yes" candidates, compare that number to what you expected from this school. If you have too many or too few call-back candidates, it may reflect the quality of the students you saw. If someone else from your organization also handled an interview schedule at this school, compare rankings and see if some individual adjustments are warranted. If your schedule was superior to your fellow interviewers', consider moving the top one or two names from your "maybe" list to your "yes" list.

FOLLOW UP

Contact every student you interviewed by letter or phone within two to three weeks after your on-campus interview. For those you are inviting for a second interview, indicate whom they should contact in your company to arrange a suitable date. Be considerate of those you are turning down: one of them may be the roommate or best friend of your most promising candidate. Word travels quickly about the way companies treat students.

SUMMARY

On-campus interviews are the most taxing interview experience you are likely to encounter. The challenges of screening top young talent coming into the job market have been compounded by the extensive interview preparation of today's candidates. The time constraints of brief interviews and the pressures of a full and intensive day add to an interviewer's stress. To get behind the resume under these circumstances, you will need to apply many of the techniques discussed throughout this book and follow the procedures outlined in this chapter. To be successful, on-campus interviewers must be thoroughly prepared, stay on schedule, handle each student with respect, and follow up on each interview within two to three weeks with a call-back invitation or a letter expressing appreciation but no interest.

23

Consultative Selling

Someone convinced against his will is of the same opinion still.

Anonymous

To hire the candidates you want, you will probably have to do some selling. The mistake most interviewers make is trying to sell the candidate too early in the interview process.

Consultative selling is borrowed from techniques skilled professionals use to convince prospective customers or clients to do business with them. It is based on mutual trust and recognition of shared interests and is carried out over a period of time beginning with the first interview. The effectiveness of consultative selling in the interview process depends on two critical factors:

1. Knowing your organization.

2. Knowing the candidate.

PREPARATION

To effectively sell a candidate on your organization, you must know its strengths and weaknesses. The best source of this kind of information is your most recently hired employees—those that have joined your organization during the last several years. In an approach similar to the one cited in Chapter 7 for gathering pluses and minuses for statements about corporate culture, ask your more recently hired employees to tell you the major reasons why they decided to become part of your company.

Ask them what unexpected benefits they have encountered since they began working in your organization. Ask what concerns they had about accepting the offer and whether those concerns proved valid. One of them might tell you, "I had heard this company was pretty stingy on bonuses, but with the new compensation program you just announced, I think that problem will be put to rest." Encourage them to volunteer other information that will be helpful to you in attracting other highly qualified candidates.

Try to get them to talk about their frustrations or dissatisfactions, especially if any of them are involved in campus recruiting or other selection interviews. Negatives that arise in the hiring process can come from your own disgruntled employees as well as from your competition. An employee on a candidate interview schedule may reveal his current dissatisfaction this way: "I've been here a long time, but if they keep cutting back and trying to run leaner, I'm going to think seriously about leaving. The stress we've all been under for the last year is really incredible."

When you've done your homework on your organization, you should have your current selling points well in mind and know what possible objections you may encounter.

The preparation also requires conducting the kind of revealing interviews with candidates that will let you know what it is about your company that will be especially important to the candidates you want to hire.

THE CONSULTATIVE SELLING PROCESS

Conducting effective selection interviews meshes well with the following six steps in the consultative selling process.

Establishing a Relationship

Because the focus in consultative selling is on mutual trust and respect, interviewers must remember that everything they do contributes to this. Clearly, avoiding a stress interview is important. So is candor and a friendly, relaxed interview climate. People may not do business with you if they don't sense this trust and respect. They won't come to work with you, either, if they sense they won't find the right relationship.

Determining Interest

It is important to learn what will motivate the candidate to accept a job offer. This knowledge evolves during the interview process as evidence about the motivational factor in general is gathered.

Sharing Information

What is said to the candidate about the organization and the job should be tailored to respond to what has been learned about the candidate's motivation and interests. Generic benefits are not nearly as convincing as information that is relevant to the candidate's specific needs.

Active acceptance by the candidate of what your organization has to offer begins at this point in the process. The selling can be enhanced by preceding information statements with questions such as, "Are you interested in learning marketing as well as selling? With our company you'll spend your first three months in our marketing department before you start sales training in the field."

A question elevates candidate interest, particularly if the question asks something that has already been learned about the candidate (e.g., that he or she has an interest in marketing as well as selling). Candidates are apt to be more receptive to selling statements that follow this type of question.

Identifying Criteria

Candidates, by the time they get to this point in the process, have determined on what basis they will accept a job offer. When they discuss these criteria with interviewers, the candidates reveal their "hot buttons." Candidates who are college recruits can be asked at this point to rank order your organization and others being considered and to state why they put them in that order. Candidates being considered from other organizations can be asked to rank order the criteria on which they will decide to change jobs.

At this point, enough information may have been exchanged between the candidate and the organization that an offer can be made. If the timing is not quite right, or there seem to be unresolved concerns, it may be necessary to move to step five. Otherwise, the process moves to step six.

Overcoming Concerns

Learning about the candidate's concerns at this stage may be critical if the offer is to be accepted. If the candidate is hesitant, but has voiced no concerns, ask him or her: "What is it about our offer that's making it difficult for you to decide to accept it now?" If the candidate says there are no concerns, then he or she should be encouraged to accept the offer. If there are concerns, they may surface on three levels, each of which requires a specific response.

▶ *Misunderstanding.* Something regarding the offer, job, or company is misunderstood by the candidate. The interviewer should take responsibility for changing this by stating, for example, "I must not have been clear (or mentioned) that we do let employees transfer to other locations after their first year."

▶ *Skepticism.* This is a more serious concern than the first. The response should verify that others have previously raised this issue or similar ones. This helps reassure the candidate that it isn't risky to voice concerns. If the candidate requests objective data to answer the concern, support that request and provide the desired information. A third-party source is ideal for resolving concerns at this level: "I understand your skepticism about gaining customer exposure quickly on this job. Perhaps you should speak to Fred Everest, who joined us a year ago with the same concern. You can learn directly from Fred what his experience has actually been."

If the candidate says, "I'm concerned whether someone coming into your organization at my level can really be accepted. It seems as though everyone here started in your training program right out of school," try to introduce the candidate to others who joined your company above entry level and have succeeded. It's not enough to say, "Others have joined us and found it to be no problem." Offer to arrange for the candidate to talk to a third party about this concern.

If your company is just now changing its traditional hiring patterns, offer the opportunity to talk to the human resources director or someone else in management who can explain what the company hopes to achieve by bringing in new talent at more experienced levels.

▶ *Real Drawbacks.* This is a substantial concern that can't be ignored. Try to get the candidate to consider the drawback in relation to the aspects of the job he or she likes. "I know you are concerned about the work this may entail on weekends, but given your career interest in learning the hospitality business and the respect you have for our organization and the people you've met, I hope you'll consider our offer in the total context of all I know is important to you in your next job." Or you may say , "I know the salary figure we discussed is only a modest bump over what you are now earning, but we think the bonus opportunity will help offset that. Further, if you consider all you are seeking in your next career move, I think you'll find overall that we still deliver better on the rest of them. Salary tends to take care of itself over time."

Reaching Agreement

This is the final step in the process, at which point the offer is extended (if it has not been extended previously) and accepted.

APPLYING CONSULTATIVE SELLING

This type of selling has two important aspects that rely on proper timing. First, the establishment of a relationship with the candidate begins when you meet for the first time. The suggestions for establishing the interview climate in Chapter 8 will help you do this.

Second, the basic model for conducting an interview calls for first assessing, then selling. Interviewers must decide when they know enough about the candidate to shift the emphasis.

Many experienced interviewers in our seminars believe you must sell almost immediately, especially in the competitive situations faced on campuses at top schools. When they learn the concepts behind consultative selling, they see that they really can't sell candidates until they know them.

One of the questions today's candidates are likely to ask in interviews is, "What are the major disadvantages of working here?" Interviewers' careful preparation can lead to a response that will help them keep the selling initiative. Interviewers should qualify their responses to such questions by saying they can answer based on their own perceptions only. They should avoid revealing a laundry list of corporatewide disadvantages. Instead, the response should begin with positives about the organization.

"Major disadvantages? Well, I suppose we have a few, as every company does. Of course, I can only comment on those I see here in the marketing department. But first let me tell you what I like about the company, because that's much more important to me and should be to you, too. What I like is the caliber of people I work with in every function across the organization. We hire top talent in every department, and that always keeps me on my toes. I also like the fact that we are pretty informal in our day-to-day working relationships—you could never say a company this size is stuffy or bureaucratic. One weakness that bothers me is that our location makes it difficult for me at this stage to be included in meetings with our advertising agency in New York. My boss and the more senior people in our brand group get to make those trips."

Another approach is to qualify a negative factor as a positive from the interviewer's perspective:

"One thing some people might consider a negative is the drill we go through to write very crisp, to-the-point memos on programs we recommend up the line. To me it's not really a negative. From my perspective I've learned a practical discipline I never acquired in school. And it's a skill I can use for the rest of my career."

FINAL THOUGHTS ON SELLING

At an early point in my career I received advice from a supervisor about managing my career. Jack McArdle told me about the three-paycheck theory, and I find it can be used convincingly to sell a candidate on your job offer.

Jack's theory is that every job provides you with three paychecks. The first is represented by your salary. The second is related to how you answer the question, "Is your current job one where you are growing and developing professionally?" If it is, that's another paycheck. The third paycheck is defined by how you answer this question: "Do you like, respect, and trust the people you work for?" If so, that's another paycheck.

Jack's advice was to be careful about changing jobs just to correct one of these three paychecks. He pointed out that if you switch jobs simply for more money, you may find your new employer milking your experience, and you won't continue to grow and develop. Or you may find you don't like or respect the people you must now work for. You wake up every morning with a knot in your stomach at the thought of going to work. You've paid a big price to increase just one paycheck!

He was quick to add that if two of your three paychecks are out of balance, you should think carefully about staying where you are. It's probably no longer a rewarding job for you.

How does this relate to selling a candidate you want to hire? If the salary you can offer is limited, point out to the candidate that there are advantages that represent two other paychecks. The candidate's concern about the size of the dollar paycheck may evaporate when the other two paychecks are described.

SUMMARY

Consultative selling is a focused technique you can use to help convert your job offers into acceptances. It is especially appropriate for the methods outlined in this book because they encourage establishing the proper relationship with the candidate throughout the interview process.

24

Using Interview Skills In Performance Appraisal

One way to let people know how they are doing is through performance appraisal and some organizations have well-developed, elaborate appraisal programs. But, many bosses hate doing appraisals. It takes time away from running the department (many think of appraisals as special projects and not part of managing), appraisals are hard to do, and it is uncomfortable to sit down with someone face-to-face and give them criticism or even praise.*

William N. Yeomans
1000 Things You Never Learned in Business School

As essential as performance appraisal is to productivity and professional growth, few managers or employees approach the process with eagerness. The task can be easier, and more constructive, when the methods presented in this book are extended to both informal and formal performance evaluations. This chapter explains how the Interview Model can enhance the performance appraisal process.

INTERVIEWING TECHNIQUES IN INFORMAL EVALUATIONS

A recent trend in performance appraisals has been to encourage ongoing informal evaluation as a supplement and prelude to

---

*William N. Yeomans, *1000 Things You Never Learned in Business School* (New York: New American Library, 1984).

formal appraisal sessions. *The One Minute Manager*, the best-selling book by Kenneth Blanchard and Spencer Johnson, supports the ongoing appraisal method through its "One Minute Praisings" and "One Minute Reprimands." These techniques encourage managers to give immediate feedback on performance that is good as well as that which is disappointing.

One Minute Praisings are based on the idea that if you encourage people by catching them in the act of doing something right, they will continue to improve their performance. One Minute Reprimands criticize the behavior, not the person, and are done immediately after the problem occurs. By providing feedback in this way, managers can prevent what Blanchard and Johnson call "gunnysack" discipline, in which managers "store up observations of poor behavior and then some day when performance review comes or they are angry in general because the sack is so full, they charge in and dump everything on the table."

Both Topic-Opener and Self-Appraisal questions can be used in the informal appraisal process. You can use the Topic-Opener to open an informal session in which to praise or reprimand the employee. Imagine one of your employees has come to a meeting with you and is not adequately prepared to answer the questions she is asked. You have to cover for the employee a great deal during the meeting, and you're upset by her lack of preparation.

Instead of going back to your office and dwelling on it—tucking it away to mention during the formal appraisal process—go to the employee's office and ask her for a few minutes. Be sure you have privacy. Then say, "You were very unprepared this morning. You had not done the data sheets, and I felt embarrassed for our team when you did not have the answers. I also was upset that you were not ready for such an important meeting. It put us in an awkward place with the other managers. I really don't understand how you could have done something like this—you are always so well prepared. *Tell me what happened regarding your preparation for this morning's meeting.*"

This question will give the employee an opportunity to tell you what got in the way of being ready. Also, while you have expressed your displeasure about the incident, you have also given her an opportunity to explain what happened—and you have assured her that the reason you are unhappy is that you have come to expect more from her. By talking about the problem immediately, you clear the air and remove the tension between you.

Similarly, if the employee has done an exceptional job presenting material in the meeting, the manager might say, "I want you to know how pleased I was with the way you delivered your report during that meeting. You were concise, specific, thorough, and handled each question well. *Tell me how you were able to prepare so well with such a tight deadline.*"

The Self-Appraisal Question also has application in the informal appraisal process. If, in the same meeting, one of your employees does a superb job in handling a difficult co-worker, let the employee know that you were pleased with his performance. Immediately after the meeting, ask him to come into your office. Then say, "I was impressed with the way you handled Ellen this morning in that meeting. You really got the meeting back on track. I notice that is a real skill of yours. *What is it about you or your previous training that enables you to handle such difficult people so easily?*"

If the situation were one in which your employee was the one who had been difficult in the meeting and you wanted to reprimand her, you might use the following Self-Appraisal Question: "You really were having a difficult time during that meeting. That's quite unlike you. *What was it about Jack—or the meeting itself—that made you resist everything that was suggested?*"

Ongoing performance appraisal, using these questioning techniques, can help reduce the tension of the yearly or twice-yearly formal evaluation interview.

INTERVIEWING TECHNIQUES IN FORMAL APPRAISALS

Several of the techniques presented in this book can also be applied to the formal appraisal process.

Setting the Climate for the Performance Appraisal Interview

It is essential that the performance appraisal interview be conducted in a way that gives the employee the feeling that he or she is being treated with interest and respect. No matter how many such appraisal sessions an employee has had, he or she arrives with some anxiety. It is therefore important to relax the employee, much as you would relax a candidate coming to your office for an interview. Some of the techniques described in Chapter 8 can be applied to the formal appraisal interview, and should be selected based on your knowledge of and relationship to the employee.

There is a trend toward focusing on the positive in formal appraisals. This trend may be an outgrowth of concerns about productivity in American industry and subsequent evaluations of systems for reinforcing performance. The result of these evaluations was summarized in *In Search of Excellence;* Peters and Waterman cite one of the qualities of excellent companies as having appraisal processes where most people can win.

Your purpose in conducting the appraisal interview is to let the employee know your evaluation of recent performance and to receive the employee's response to your evaluation. This should be a time for agreeing on strategies to improve performance, setting new objectives, and creating opportunities for continued professional growth. Even if some of the issues discussed may be difficult for both manager and employee, setting the right climate can help establish a positive focus.

If you and the employee begin the appraisal interview with small talk, use a signal similar to the one you use in a selection interview to let the employee know it's time to get on with the performance appraisal. And, just as you let the candidate do most of the talking in a selection interview, you'll want to encourage the employee to talk in this appraisal interview. You should also ask the employee to prepare a self-appraisal, which you receive before or at the beginning of the appraisal interview.

Applying the Interview Model

When employees are given the opportunity to talk about their performance, you gain valuable insights and confirm behavioral premises much as you do in a selection interview. Use a Topic-Opener to begin the interview with the candidate, "Your department has had another good quarter, and you have contributed greatly to that productivity. Tell me about the satisfactions and challenges you have experienced over the past six months." Listen, and give verbal and nonverbal acceptance as the employee is talking.

Follow up with questions that probe the employee's accom-plishments and ask some Self-Appraisal questions: "Although I have worked closely with you during this period, I'd be interested to know what you think it was about your work that led to the increased profit margin on that product?" or "What was it about your manage-ment of the project that enabled you to deliver that design on time and under budget?"

Continue the model by asking one or more Situation-Based questions. "I remember that during the last production run you were troubled by Alex's carelessness about safety measures on the line. You seem to have resolved that problem effectively. Of the several measures you tried, which do you think worked?" If there has been a change in the supervision responsibility or the composition of the work group, ask a Comparison question. "You've been supervising your new work group now for five months, and doing a good job. Looking back on your previous work group, how would you compare the challenges you have faced with each?"

You can discuss limitations in the appraisal interview and still keep the focus on the positive. You know that an employee is a combination of many qualities and strengths as well as limitations. After you have focused extensively on the positive, try to get the employee to talk about his or her limitations.

It is far better to let the employee bring up perceived shortcom-ings before you bring up the areas for improvement that you have observed. "Although your productivity has improved greatly since our last session, I'd like you to tell me where you think you need to improve in order to further increase your contribution to the depart-ment's output."

Using the model suggested in the structure of the selection interview, you should time these questions so they come after there has been considerable discussion about the positive growth and contributions of the employee. If the employee is reluctant to talk about shortcomings or areas in need of improvement, use some of the other techniques presented in Chapter 14 for probing limitations.

If there are discrepancies between your appraisal of the candidate and the candidate's oral or written self-appraisal, confront that discrepancy directly. The technique is similar to introducing stress into a selection interview. Say to the candidate after the interview is well underway and you have discussed positive accomplishments, "In reviewing your self-appraisal of your performance, I noted that you rated yourself much higher in delegation than I have. Tell me more about how you see your strengths in delegating, and give me a few examples of the situations you were thinking of when you rated yourself." The employee then will have to come up with the facts to verify his or her assessment in this area.

Dealing with the Poor Performer

While the majority of the performance appraisal interviews you conduct should emphasize the positive, there will be some where the news is not good. Employees should not have to wait until a performance appraisal interview to hear that they are not succeeding in their jobs. It is important to deal with poor performance as soon as it happens. "The One Minute Reprimand" approach is one way to deal with the poor performer. To delay intervention can create problems for the individual, his or her work group, and the organization. Poor performance is demoralizing for others and can reduce overall productivity.

Often, the intervention must be quick and therefore not as well thought out as a performance appraisal interview you plan and conduct in a relaxed atmosphere. However, as a follow-up to the immediate intervention, schedule an interview with the employee and use some elements of the interview model to get the employee to talk about his or her problems.

Use a Topic Opener: "Tell me about the problems you are having in this job." If the candidate is reluctant, you can cite the incident(s) in which you or others have had to intervene. Ask a Self-Appraisal Question: "What do you think it is about your performance that is leading to the difficulty you have been having?" Finally, ask some Situation-Based Questions to further clarify the problem.

The discussion growing out of this kind of unscheduled performance appraisal interview can reveal a great deal, particularly if the employee is a recent hire. Perhaps the employee really had a different idea about what was expected and what would be offered. Perhaps there was inadequate orientation. An employee who consistently comes in a half-hour late may never have been told what time the work day starts, or that your company considers punctuality important.

Try to find out the reasons during this interview. At the end of the session, be sure you have resolved all the misunderstandings and set some performance goals for the employee. If the problems seem to be present still, be definite about what will happen with the employee from this point forward in terms of probation, suspension, and change in work group or work place, and let the employee know that you value his or her employment in your organization and want to work to resolve these problems.

SUMMARY

Performance appraisals can benefit from many of the same techniques as effective selection interviews. For ongoing informal appraisals—both positive and negative—the Topic-Opener and Self-Appraisal questions can help managers provide immediate feedback and increase employee acceptance of the process. For formal appraisal interviews, techniques for relaxing the interview climate and employing the interview model will make this somewhat difficult task more productive for both manager and employee.

25

Hiring Professionals

*Law schools tend to be a special event where intellectual and academic skills are paramount. Law practice requires a decathlon of skills.**

Samuelson Reports

The power of the Interview Model and of the techniques presented in *Getting Behind the Resume* lies in their easy application to nearly all organizational hiring situations. Because each interview is based on the qualities desired for that particular position ranged against the situational influences on the job and the organization's culture, the model can be fine-tuned to fit a wide variety of situations. This chapter makes some general observations on using the model in specialized professional organizations: it also details how the various techniques can be used in a specific professional setting—the lawyer-selection interview.

*Don S. Samuelson, *Samuelson Reports* (Chicago).

FOCUS ON THE PERFORMANCE FACTORS

One of the greatest tendencies in hiring for technical or specialized professional positions is to overestimate the importance of the Resume Factor when evaluating candidates. This issue, which is explored throughout this book, can't be emphasized enough. Although law firms, accounting firms, architectural firms, engineering consulting firms, software developers, and other similar organizations must depend on the technical expertise of each professional employee, they must also recognize the importance of behavioral factors in predicting a person's success in their organization.

This is particularly true in small organizations, where each employee interacts with all other employees, and where each person is expected to carry a fairly large share of the workload. If an employee's Performance Factors—Intellectual, Interpersonal, and Motivational—aren't thoroughly assessed against a pre-established set of criteria, hiring mistakes can be made which can have damaging effects on the entire organization.

The Resume Factor must be assessed to see if the person qualifies for the open position. However, once this initial screening has taken place, the focus should be on using the techniques for exploring the Performance Factors. These include using facts and accomplishments from the resume and the interview itself to find out not only *what* the person did but *how* he or she accomplished it. This does not mean minimizing the importance of technical qualifications when considering a candidate. It does mean putting those technical qualifications into the larger context of the candidate's total potential fit with the job. When interviews are conducted using the behavioral model, the candidate evaluations and recommendations will provide much richer information about the candidate. Consider these two different recommendations on a candidate for an engineering position:

1. We should hire Tom because he has an excellent academic record behind his EE degree and he's got the three years' experience we are looking for in designing engineering standards that are required to control and develop our software program.

2. Tom is qualified academically and has relevant design experi-

ence. Our work should be self-motivating to him because it is in an area of his special interest. He has demonstrated he can handle stress similar to what he'll experience here. His pattern as a team player will help him fit into our work culture.

Both descriptions of Tom acknowledge his match with functional job requirements (degree type and years of specific job experience). However, the second one also predicts a behavioral fit with the job.

Specialized professional and technical organizations must make special efforts not to place too much emphasis on technical competency and ignore the key Performance Factors that can insure a candidate's fit with their organizations.

USE THE INTERVIEW MODEL AND TOPIC AREAS

The focus on the Resume Factor is a direct outgrowth of the traditional focus on the resume itself in technical or specialized professional interviewing. The interviewer looks for certain key experience and education factors and frequently spends the entire interview verifying and discussing information stated on the resume. Using the resume as a prop is particularly risky in this kind of technical interviewing because interviewer and interviewee have a common language of professional and academic buzzwords that can obscure the important aspects of a candidate's qualifications for the position.

By using topic areas (such as education, current job, and previous jobs) to guide the flow of the interview, instead of the item-by-item listing on the resume, interviewers can move through education and experience in a nonchronological order, breaking what has probably been a practiced pattern for the interviewee. The Interview Model (see Chapter 9), applies three basic question formats to as many as six topic areas and can require candidates to rethink and restate certain answers that they had practiced before the interview. In this way, greater insights into what a candidate is really like can be gained. In short, interviewers will get behind the resume.

LISTENING

The need for technical and academic exchange in specialized and technical professions is part of the job. Therefore, there is a tendency in this type of interviewing for the interviewer to do too much talking. Because the focus is on the technical, and the interviewer wants to let the interviewee know that the company knows what it's doing, the interviewer may try to dazzle the candidate with a display of proficiency in the subject area or discipline. There is plenty of time for that after the person is hired. The purpose of this interview is to find out what the candidate has done, how he or she has done it, and what he or she knows. Therefore, the 80/20 listening rule applies in this type of interviewing as well: the interviewer should listen 80 percent of the time.

DECISION-MAKING PROCESS

Excellent candidates who lack the exact education and experience set forth in many technical and professional job descriptions are frequently passed over in the selection process. This happens because interviewers do not know how to look at the entire range of strengths and limitations a candidate possesses and how to balance a shortcoming in one area with a strength in another. In Chapter 18, the importance of learning to weigh experience and aptitude is discussed. This is particularly important when evaluating candidates for technical or professional positions. A candidate with just four of the requisite five years experience for a particular position may nonetheless exhibit an aptitude and have potential that will quickly make up for this shortcoming.

Also, people with high intellectual capacity and ability to apply it have little trouble learning more about a new discipline or technical area. And, if the candidate's interest in the area is high, his or her motivation will help accomplish the learning that will have to take place. A candidate with less experience but greater aptitude, interest, and enthusiasm may be preferable to a candidate who exceeds the experience requirements but lacks the motivation or intellectual discipline to grow with the job.

254

CONSULTATIVE SELLING

Candidates with superior education, experience, and performance are highly sought by professional and technical organizations. Most interviewers from these organizations think they can tell by looking at the resume whether they want to hire the person. Indeed, much can be inferred from the resume. But the resume is just the beginning.

No matter how qualified the candidate appears on paper, it is still important to conduct a revealing interview before trying to sell the candidate on the organization. The best selling occurs after the interviewing organization has had an opportunity to "read" the motivation factor in highly qualified candidates. This happens only when effective interviews are conducted. By allowing the interview(s) to reveal the interests, goals, and overall motivation of top candidates, the organization has a better opportunity to offer the position in a way that will tap into that motivation and increase the likelihood of acceptance. It is greatly to the organization's advantage to put off selling the candidate until these essential aspects of the candidate's interests are assessed. The steps in Consultative Selling (Chapter 23) are particularly appropriate for technical and professional firms.

ATTORNEY SELECTION

Attorney selection interviewing provides special opportunities for applying the interviewing process presented in *Getting Behind the Resume*. Lawyers spend hundreds of hours interviewing prospective new associates. Yet most lawyers with considerable interviewing experience have had little of the kind of interviewing training that can make selection interviews for potential associates or lateral hires more effective.

Increasingly, law firms, legal departments, government agencies, and other organizations that employ attorneys are interviewing candidates who have had excellent coaching and counseling by their law school placement offices and are extremely well-prepared for the interview process. Career planning and placement services provided by the law schools give candidates the opportunity to have their resumes evaluated, participate in practice interview sessions (usually with videotape), receive constructive feedback on their interviewing techniques, and have post-interview review sessions while they are in the job-seeking process.

Students also have access to comments on file in the placement office from other students who may have served in these firms as summer associates, and can read the annual survey of student evaluations printed in *The American Lawyer.* Firm resumes, from which they can gain valuable information about the firm's culture, are also readily obtained. It is easy for these well-prepared candidates to take control of the interview.

Another challenge that attorneys face in selection interviewing is in the kinds of questioning techniques they tend to use. Revealing interviews occur when open-ended questions are asked and when interviewers refrain from telegraphing answers. This runs counter to the way many lawyers must interview in their handling of interrogations, depositions, and court trials. The interviewing approach that is powerful in the courtroom is limiting in the selection process. Many lawyers have to dramatically shift their techniques when interviewing a candidate for a position in their firm or organization. The techniques suggested in this book can assist hiring attorneys in making this required shift.

The tendency in lawyer hiring has always been to go for the person with top grades who has been on law review. In working with law firms and other organizations employing a staff of attorneys, we urge them to give weight to other qualities as well. The Interview Model is a helpful and productive tool for them in going beyond the Resume Factor and really considering the Performance Factors.

The rest of this chapter will outline how to apply these techniques through the interview cycle.

Prepare for the Recruiting Season

Before beginning the annual recruitment season, many law firms, law departments, and other organizations assess their recruitment practices and reevaluate the success factors among attorneys in their organizations. They tend to hire from the same specifications each year, not looking at the situational influences that may have affected the firm since the last recruiting season or anticipated changes that will affect the people they decide to hire. The increasing presence of professional recruitment coordinators in larger law firms has done much to strengthen and systematize the recruitment and hiring process in these firms. Chapter 7, "The Candidate/Job Profile," describes a system for developing more complete descriptions for hiring.

On-Campus Interviews

On-campus interviews are discussed thoroughly in Chapter 22. All the techniques and advice in that chapter can be used by attorneys who conduct on-campus interviews. Of particular interest is the information on the need to focus on the motivation factor as a way of narrowing the candidate field among those who have impressive resumes. With the suggested ratio of listening to talking (70/30), in a 20-minute campus interview the candidate will be talking approximately 14 minutes. This leaves limited time for small talk and some closing comments by the interviewer, and a brief opportunity for the interviewer to talk about the firm or try to sell the candidate.

In this screening process, attorneys should look beyond grades and law review to "read" a candidate's potential contribution. They should look for interesting summer work, special course work, evidence of a variety (or intensity) of interests, and other accomplishments that indicate a person who may be of value to the firm or organization. In the interview, conducted using the Interview Model, interviewing attorneys should be open and accepting even with candidates who on paper don't appear to have the credentials the interviewer is looking for. While the interviewee may not be someone in whom the firm will be interested, the news of rude or insensitive treatment by on-campus interviewers has a way of getting around, and a firm or organization may lose a candidate they *do* want because of their treatment of a candidate they did *not* want.

It is particularly important in this setting not to jump to conclusions about candidates (particularly before meeting them) and to look for the person who may be a positive contributor to your firm. Interviewers may find that a person's class standing was affected by having to work to support a family, or by an illness or other factor beyond his or her control. If that information emerges during the interview (which it probably will, because the candidate will want the interviewer to know about it) this could be the first piece of data from the interviewee that will lead to an eventual conclusion by the interviewer that he or she is hard-working, self-disciplined, and mature.

Those qualities can be more important than grades or law review. There is instance after instance of bright young attorneys with impeccable credentials who didn't make partner. Most often, the reasons for not making it tied back to the Performance Factors: they didn't work hard enough (a motivational factor), they weren't persuasive with clients (interpersonal), they didn't take the initiative (motivational), they got buried in analysis before making decisions (intellectual), or fell short in other non-Resume Factors.

Like on-campus interviewers hiring for any kind of organization, interviewers for law firms should guard against arranging call-back interviews with candidates who are not likely to be hired. The reasons for this are reviewed in Chapter 22, and should be read over by interviewers planning their on-campus interview program.

Use a limited amount of your 20-minute interview time for selling the firm to the candidate during this interview. Insufficient information about the candidate's interests, goals, motivation, and overall Performance Factors can lead to hiring mistakes.

If the candidate turns out to be one the firm wants to hire, and if the candidate is interested in working for the firm, there will be time during the call-back interviews to do some selling. Do just enough selling on campus to sustain the student's interest and to insure acceptance of a call-back interview. Chapter 23 on Consultative Selling provides strong evidence for the value of saving the sell until there is ample knowledge about what the candidate wants.

The Call-Back Interview

Applying the Interview Model to call-back interviews in the firm or legal department allows interviewers the opportunity to explore and confirm inferences made during the on-campus interview and gather information that will lead to verification of key behavioral premises about the candidate.

Consistent with the Interview Model, attorneys conducting the interviews should open with a Topic-Opener Question. The one used most often among the attorneys we work with is "Let's talk about your law school years." Where appropriate, interviewers might also say, "Tell me about your work on Law Review," or "Tell me about your work as a summer associate." These broad questions give candidates a chance to select, organize, and articulate their relevant experience.

The interview must not be just a fact-gathering mission which verifies the information on the resume. Interviewers will use the information gathered that relates to the Resume Factor to begin to draw inferences about the candidate's Performance Factors. The Self-Appraisal Question helps draw out this information. The following dialogue shows how a Self-Appraisal Question can be used in an interview with a potential associate.

Q.—I suppose you are looking forward to completing law school and starting work with a firm.

A.—That's absolutely right. I can't wait to get out of school, throw myself into my work, and begin to get some real experience.

Q.—Did your work last summer in the local District Attorney's office influence the way you now feel?

A.—Yes, it did. It was a taste of the real world for me.

Q. (Self-Appraisal Question)—What was it about that work that you particularly enjoyed?

A.—I got some quick experience in the DA's office. They were short-handed last summer, and I had to pick up 10 cases and sort of had to teach myself just to keep my head above water.

Q. (Self-Appraisal Question)—Why was that so enjoyable for you?

A.—It was so different from law school and really challenged me in some new ways. It was all very exciting—I had so much to do—I even found myself reading briefs on the elevator on the way to the courtroom. I really had to do things fast and was under great pressure to perform.

This particular illustration generates lively discussion in our selection interviewing seminars for lawyers. There is a strong difference of opinion regarding the potential fit of this young man in any one firm. People who applaud the last answer admire the self-starting qualities reflected in the response. Those with concerns wonder if the person will work only under pressure and be careless as well (reading legal briefs in an elevator!). Clearly, both sides would have more to follow up on in the balance of the interview.

An example such as this illustrates the value of asking Self-Appraisal Questions. The fact that the law student worked the previous summer in the DA's office does not mean a great deal by itself. It's in the probing of the nature of the experience that behavioral premises emerge.

Situation-Based Questions also provide information and insights about how well candidates will fit into the particular legal setting for which they are interviewing. Problem-Situation questions can be posed that frame problems which the interviewer knows an associate will confront, but which the candidate may feel are hypothetical. When the interviewer is careful not to telegraph the desired answer, the candidate's response can provide valuable behavioral insights.

The interviewer can ask, "How would you handle a situation in which a client expects you to be "on call" like a doctor, day and night, even when the problems aren't very important and could wait until the next day?"

The interviewer knows that this exactly describes a client this person could be working with, but the candidate would answer it in the abstract. "It's important to me to establish a good relationship with a client, and so I would try to be available whenever the client needed me. However, I would hope that the client would respect my time and realize that I prefer to handle these normal problems during the work day—but would always be ready to deal with a major problem at any time."

Or the candidate might say, "I would try to make it clear at the outset that my time away from the office is valuable and that I want to handle such problems during office hours. I suppose if it were really important I would want to deal with it, but otherwise things like that can wait until Monday."

These two responses will mean different things to the interviewer, depending on the situation. If the law firm has been looking for someone who can deal strongly yet diplomatically with a client who abuses their attorneys' personal time, they may prefer the candidate who would take a tough stand. However, this may be a very valued client who provides a substantial portion of the firm's annual revenue. The firm would be reluctant to put an attorney on the client team who would not be receptive to weekend and evening calls. Another inference that could be made, depending on the client and the setting, is that the first attorney might be too accommodating and may have problems handling several clients who try to have such privileges.

The value of behavioral insights gained is directly related to the interviewer's understanding of what is important to the job.

The topics suggested for use with the Interview Model can also be adapted for lawyer selection interviewing. Some examples were given in the section on the Topic-Opener Question. While some hiring attorneys prefer not to spend much time talking about the candidate's undergraduate college years, we recommend that these years and experiences not be overlooked as a rich source of material for drawing out and verifying information about the Performance Factors. When interviewers consider the *meaning* of an accomplishment as it gives insight into *how* someone will do a job, *when* the accomplishment occurred doesn't matter as much. A candidate who has shown leadership qualities and organizational ability in law school will probably have shown those same qualities in college and even in high school. The more ways in which interviewers can confirm behavioral inferences, the more value they will have in the decision-making process. Repeated evidence of certain qualities will help interviewers be more confident that they have selected the right person.

At the conclusion of the round of in-firm interviews, the decision-making process described in Chapter 18 should be followed. There are no special instructions for attorneys, only that those making the hiring decision remember the importance of the behavioral or Performance Factors as well as the Resume Factor when making the decision. More than likely, the candidates selected to receive offers will be selected by other firms as well. In that case, selling must take place.

Consultative Selling

Consultative selling, covered in Chapter 23, is an essential strategy for hiring attorneys. Most law firms, law departments, and governmental agencies compete for top candidates and therefore must know how to sell the benefits of working for their particular organization. The material provided in Chapter 23 will provide attorneys with the skills needed to carry out this process. However, the following points deserve emphasis in the context of legal hiring:

● The competition for top candidates should not push the firm or organization into trying to sell candidates too early in the interviewing cycle. Interviewers must save the sell until they understand the candidate's interests, goals, and other motivating drives. Premature selling is usually based on the wrong points. To hit the "hot buttons" that will make a candidate come to work for a particular organization, an interviewer must know what the candidate wants.

● The consultative selling time is a time for candor. The sought-after candidate is a person the firm has decided they want to work with for many years. To obscure information or realities that will prevent the candidate from being satisfied with the firm is unfair to the candidate and unfair to the firm. The person will not stay if the true conditions are such that being with this organization will not be challenging or satisfying.

● When confronting a serious drawback that can't be resolved, it's best to let the candidate go. As mentioned above, when organizations try to gloss over reality, the likelihood is that the associate will begin looking for another position before long.

● Interviewers should anticipate a candidate's possible objections before they are expressed. This clears the way for an open discussion of what the firm really has to offer. For example, in some cities some law firms tell candidates negatives about other firms to discourage them from accepting positions offered by the competition. This information can be misleading. A recent conversation with an attorney from one firm and a director of human resources from another focused on this issue. In both firms, this issue is raised early in the selling process. "You may have heard that our firm . . . and we just wanted you to know that is not true. In fact, our firm . . ." It is important in this exchange with a candidate not to feed the rumor mill and to omit mentioning where they might have heard such information. At this level of possible objection, a third-party opinion (see material in Chapter 23 on overcoming skepticism) is usually helpful in convincing the candidate that what he or she has heard is not true.

● Consultative selling is dignified and based on mutual respect. Hard-sell tactics are incompatible with this approach, but enthusiasm is encouraged. The best sell a firm has is the satisfaction and enthusiasm of the interviewers each candidate meets.

SUMMARY

The Interview Model is simple and flexible enough to be used in a wide variety of organizations. Some of its techniques are particularly relevant to selecting professionals, where an inordinate amount of weight is generally given to the Resume Factor. The importance of getting behind the resume is particularly important in lawyer-selection interviewing, where the candidates are exceptionally well-prepared and the pool of top applicants is shrinking. Behavioral interviewing offers organizations ways to expand the hiring criteria without compromising quality and potential in the professionals they hire.

26

Use by the Human Resources Function

Most companies have very workable processes for hiring the best people available and good correlation with success requirements for the initial job. But leader companies have developed more elaborate profiles—some of them fact-based, some built around company culture and lore. They identify, with uncanny success, the type of personnel appropriate to their institutions.*

David McLaughlin
Strategic Human Resources Management

The implementation of the interviewing process described in this book has a twofold significance for human resources professionals. Most HR professionals have had considerable interview training and conduct interviews regularly as part of their jobs. The value of *Getting Behind the Resume* lies therefore not only in whatever new techniques or strategies *they* learn about interviewing, but in how they can help *line managers* learn and apply them.

For experienced human resources professionals, the concepts and techniques presented in this book can enhance their effective support of line managers during the hiring process. When human resources professionals discuss open jobs in behavioral terms and help managers create candidate/job profiles that capture the duties,

---

*David McLaughlin, "The Turning Point in Human Resources Management," as published in *Strategic Human Resources Management*.

culture, and desired qualities that describe the job, their analysis and expertise can complement the technical expertise of the line managers. Then there is a common basis for discussion of candidates that is not limited to technical qualifications.

Most line managers have had little or no interviewing training, and many do little interviewing. The challenges they face and the mistakes they often make are described in Chapters 1 and 2 of this book. Because today's job *candidates* are well-prepared for every interview, a key function of the human resources department in any organization should be to help prepare *interviewers* to conduct more effective interviews.

Here are several specific strategies human resources professionals can use to add real value to the service role of helping line managers fill jobs.

PREPARING THE CANDIDATE/JOB PROFILE

This profile (see Chapter 7) is the backdrop against which interviewing and candidate evaluation takes place. Its preparation is a strategic step in the hiring process, and one in which human resources professionals can participate with line management. By working closely with the hiring manager(s) in the development of the profile, HR professionals can supply key information about the job, help the manager define the cultural factors that affect the job, and determine which Resume and Performance Factors will be sought.

In defining the job and the culture, human resources professionals can add the perspective of the overall organization to the information the line manager supplies about the specific departmental or job needs and environment. These two elements are then combined for a comprehensive summary of the duties and culture, creating a candidate/job profile that supports the interviewing process and candidate evaluation.

For the selection of the behavioral factors, the HR professional should supply a list of qualities consistent with the overall culture of the organization from which the manager can choose ones that are most appropriate for the open position. In the preparation of this profile, situational influences on the job should be considered, including job history, anticipated changes, co-workers and other factors.

All support materials used in the hiring process should be revised to be compatible with the focus and terminology of the candidate/job profile. These materials would include the job requisition, the interview write-up sheet or balance sheet, and other documents required by the hiring process. Line managers should be provided with these materials and instructed in their use.

SOURCING AND SCREENING CANDIDATES

As a result of working with the hiring manager on the candidate/job profile, the HR professional will have a much stronger set of criteria to use when sourcing and screening candidates. In the screening process, the HR professional will find the Interview Model works well. In particular, the topic approach and questioning techniques will enable the screening interviewer to find out much more about each candidate and make better recommendations to the hiring managers.

This is especially true when interviewing candidates for positions where the technical specifications are outside the HR professional's expertise. The interview model enables nontechnical interviewers to gather information about behavioral qualities that can provide good insights into the candidate's potential for success in the organization.

INTERVIEWING

In addition to the management of tasks associated with the interviewing process, human resources professionals should take a proactive role as part of the candidate evaluation team. This role begins with the screening interview itself. Information from the screening interviews with each candidate, evaluated in the context of the candidate/job profile, should be given to each interviewer well enough in advance for review and discussion. Interviewers then should be provided with the support materials for the interview process. In particular, they should be shown how to synthesize the behavioral premises from their notes and record them on the balance sheet as soon as possible after the interview.

PROVIDING A SUPPORT SYSTEM

The human resources manager can help line managers integrate these interviewing concepts into a company-wide system. The HR function is the natural focal point in a company for achieving this, and it is relatively simple to do. Components of such a system include the following:

▶ *Requisition.* This incorporates all the elements described in the Candidate/Job Profile and adds to it the necessary approvals to initiate the process that results in a job being filled in a company. When done in this manner, the initial discussion and agreement on desired candidate qualities centers on all four factors necessary to consider for on-the-job success. A sample requisition follows.

▶ *Candidate evaluation.* This captures the assessment of each person who interviewed the candidate. It follows the balance sheet format described in Chapter 18. A sample balance sheet follows, printed on two sides of a single sheet. The reverse side provides suggestions for completing this balance sheet. This format illustrates how little is required to turn these interviewing concepts into an HR support system for company-wide application.

▶ *Interviewing schedule.* The schedule provided by HR can help control the in-company interview process and suggest individual factors to probe in depth. This can add variety to the interviews and insure that each of the four factors is covered thoroughly. A sample schedule follows.

PERSONNEL REQUISITION

TITLE _____ DEPT. _____ REQ. # _____

GRADE ___ DATE REQUIRED ___ EXEMPT ___ NON-EXEMPT ___

Position Specifications

1. Why This Job Exists (replacement? new position? part of staffing plan?)

_____

_____

2. Major Job Functions (list 5–7 in decreasing order of importance)

_____

_____

_____

_____

3. Expected Accomplishments? (Specific major objectives or key programs. Consider current priorities and future needs.)

_____

_____

_____

_____

4. Functional Relationships (who the person must work with and influence)

_____

Candidate Specifications

Considering major job functions, expected accomplishments, and working relationships, please identify some of the strengths the candidate should have against the factor listed below.

RESUME FACTOR (EDUCATION/EXPERIENCE) (e.g., degrees, certification, experience)

_____

_____

INTELLECTUAL FACTOR (e.g., analytical ability, written/verbal communications)

_____

_____

INTERPERSONAL FACTOR (e.g., leadership, team player, train others communications)

_____

_____

MOTIVATIONAL FACTOR (e.g., interests, energy type, and amount)

_____

_____

OTHER SKILLS (e.g., hand and measurement tool capability)

_____

_____

POTENTIAL CANDIDATES/SOURCES _____

APPROVALS _____
Manager/Director   Date

_____
Vice President   Date

_____
Manager Human Resources   Date

NEW HIRE _____ START DATE _____

Use by the Human Resources Function

BALANCE SHEET

CANDIDATE EVALUATION
See reverse side for preparation guidelines.

APPLICANT: _____ POSITION: _____
INTERVIEWER: _____ DATE: _____
Recommended for Employment ___ Not Recommended _____

ESSENTIAL
FACTORS

STRENGTHS   RESUME   LIMITATIONS

(EDUCATION/EXPERIENCE)

INTELLECTUAL

INTERPERSONAL

MOTIVATIONAL

FIT WITH OUR CULTURE.

COMPLETING THE BALANCE SHEET

Here are some pointers to help you interview, then complete the front of this form. Start by identifying what you are looking for from the Requisition.

In addition to specific qualities listed on the Requisition consider:

RESUME FACTOR (EDUCATION/EXPERIENCE)

Tasks performed that evidence desirable experience. Specific technical knowledge acquired, e.g., Knowledge of electro-mechanical assemblies. Note special academic achievements. Experience supervising others. Experience in a work culture similar to ours. Trade show demonstration experience.

INTELLECTUAL

e.g., Analytical. Articulate. Problem Solver. Judgment—intellectual capacity and effective application. Decision making style—use of facts vs. intuition. Logical. Well organized.

INTERPERSONAL

e.g., Self Confident. Team Player. Dominant. Forceful. Extroverted. Outgoing. Patient. Sense of urgency. Conforming. Methodical. Leadership qualities. Good trainer. Persuasive.

MOTIVATIONAL

e.g., Job and career goals. Expected salary. Interests. Hobbies (e.g., hands on). Energy level. Type of energy (project vs. steady)

SPECIAL SKILLS

e.g., Can understand assembly instructions process sheets. Can use hand and measurement tools. Can lift boxes weighing 60 lbs. Can answer technical service inquiries over the telephone.

FIT WITH OUR CULTURE

Does candidate evidence beliefs and values similar to those held here —e.g., technical competence, commitment to excellence, high work standards, ability to interact effectively with others?

Recommended Action:

_____ Make Offer _____ No Offer _____ Retain in Active File

Interviewing Schedule

Candidate _____

Opening _____

Date _____

Time	Topic	Interviewer
9:00 - 9:30	Overview of the Day	
9:30 - 10:30	In-Depth Assessment (Also Probe Education/ Experience—Resume Factor)	
10:30 - 11:30	In-Depth Assessment (Also Probe Interpersonal)	
11:30 - 12:00	Interview	
12:00 - 1:30	Lunch	
1:30 - 2:30	In-Depth Interview (Also Probe Intellectual)	
2:30 - 3:00	Interview	
3:00 - 3:30	Interview	
3:30 - 4:00	In-Depth Interview (Also Probe Motivational)	
4:30 -	Wrap Up	

EVALUATION

In Chapter 18, the process for making the decision is described. It is a process in which HR professionals can play a key role. Briefly, the process consists of reviewing the candidate/job profile, going over interviewer notes and balance sheets, comparing balance sheets with the candidate/job profile and selecting the best candidate. If there is no clear choice, additional candidates may have to be called in or additional interviews conducted with candidates already seen.

HR professionals can contribute by keeping the decision-making process on time and focused. They can provide time and guidance in the reevaluation of the Resume and Performance Factors on the profile and the consideration of each candidate against those standards. They can show managers how to trade off strengths and limitations as they evaluate candidates, and help them avoid rejecting candidates for only one negative quality or a shortcoming in the precise requirements stated for education or experience.

The HR professional's corporate perspective can help department managers fold in larger organizational priorities in their candidate selections. Further, if there is difficulty in reaching consensus, the HR professional may be able to supply additional information that will assist others in overcoming their objections and reaching a decision.

CHALLENGES FOR HUMAN RESOURCES PROFESSIONALS

Guiding managers in the application of these interviewing strategies and techniques may present some challenges. The principal one is that many managers completely overemphasize the importance of the Resume Factor. Its importance in screening out the nonqualified can blind people to the fact that it is also the factor least likely to predict on-the-job failure. People who don't work out in a job probably have one or more of the Performance Factors working against them. Intellectually, they cannot keep up with the growing complexity of a job (or communicate effectively or make good decisions, for example). Or, interpersonally, they are not team players (or they lack persuasiveness or diplomacy). Or, motivationally, they fail to develop interests to match new developments in their specialty area or they won't put in the required hours or they lack energy to meet new job demands.

All managers and professionals can benefit from using effective behavior-based selection interviewing skills. The behavioral interviewing process helps balance the natural tendency of line managers to focus too much on technical specifications, and can help human resources professionals conduct revealing screening interviews with candidates outside their area of expertise.

Human resources professionals can take a more proactive role in interviewing and hiring an organization's most valuable resource, its people. By providing tools and training based on behavioral interviewing, HR professionals can teach line managers skills and strategies to become more effective interviewers. They can help managers get away from reliance on the Resume Factor and build confidence in the Performance Factors as predictors of on-the-job success.

SUMMARY

The interview process presented in this book provides opportunities for human resources professionals to help their organizations become one of the "leader companies" referred to by David McLaughlin at the beginning of this chapter. By providing a support system and then working in partnership with line managers, HR professionals can develop candidate/job profiles that reflect the overall goals of the organization, its culture, and the behavioral specifications for the job. They can help managers use these interviewing strategies to conduct more effective interviews with today's well-prepared candidates. Finally, they can help in the candidate evaluation process by working with line managers to insure that the behavior-based candidate/job profile is used as a guide in evaluating the information from the interview during the decision-making process.

Appendix A

Sample Candidate Job Profiles

The candidate/job profile is a key element in the planning and evaluation of a revealing interview. Its preparation, importance, and use are discussed in Chapter 7.

In the *planning* phase of the interview, the preparation of the candidate/job profile permits you and your co-workers to consider not only the duties and responsibilities of the job, but also the cultural environment in which the work will take place and the desired Resume and Performance Factors. It provides a much richer description of the job—the *how* as well as the *what*—than traditional payroll-driven job descriptions.

The candidate/job profile is developed for organizational and interviewer use, and is not a job description that is given to the candidate. It can become the basis of a company's requisition, as described in Chapter 27.

In the *evaluation* of each interview, and the process of reaching a hiring decision, the candidate/job profile will provide the standard against which you will compare the balance sheet you have prepared on each candidate. The three elements in the evaluation process—candidate/job profile, notes, and balance sheet—enable you to make an objective hiring decision.

You will want to practice developing candidate/job profiles in preparation for your next interviews. The following additional copy of the recommended format is included for your use—photocopy as needed.

Candidate/Job Profile

DUTIES

CULTURE

FACTORS:

RESUME FACTOR

- **Education/Experience**

PERFORMANCE FACTORS

- **Intellectual**

- **Interpersonal**

- **Motivational**

Appendix B

Role Play Script and Procedures

You may want to practice the techniques and strategies described in *Getting Behind the Resume* before you try them out in an actual interview. The role play script and procedures in this chapter will help you try out these new approaches to interviewing.

There are two parts to the role play preparation, the role play script and the procedures for conducting the role play. The script provides a model for conducting the role play, and contains the basic elements of the Interview Model.

You may add to it as you like (for example, to practice other techniques) or shorten it if you want only some quick practice in preparation for an interview. If you shorten the script, be sure to include a Topic Opener and a Self-Appraisal Question as a minimum. The role play procedures advise conducting the role play in groups of three, with each member trading off as interviewer, interviewee and observer. If this isn't possible—because of lack of people to practice with or lack of time—then find just one person to work with and omit the observer role. You will still benefit greatly from this exercise.

INTERVIEW ROLE PLAY SCRIPT

Interviewer Instructions

Assume the person you are interviewing is a graduating senior or experienced manager (choose one) being considered for employment in your organization. Undergraduate work was at _____ (ask the "candidate"). Assume also that you are into the interview, so you can omit the small talk if you prefer. Your goal during this role play of approximately 15 minutes is to learn as much as you can about the candidate's college years (or current job).

Script

1. Open with a Topic-Opener Question such as

"Tell me about your college years" or

"Tell me about your current job."

2. Take notes.

3. Ask follow-up questions.

4. Acknowledge accomplishments. "That's impressive that you did _____."

5. Ask one or two Self-Appraisal Questions:

"You mentioned that...."

"What, would you say, was it about you that...."

6. Ask one or two Situtation-Based Questions, selecting from the four types (Problem Situation, Continuum, Comparison, and Future Assessment).

7. Probe limitations:

"You have impressive accomplishments. What about the other side of the coin...?"

"What are some things you don't do quite so well?"

"Is there any small thing that could be improved?"

"How would you say you've grown the most in the last few years?"

PROCEDURES FOR CONDUCTING THE ROLE PLAY

If you have three willing people (including yourself) and time for a full role play practice, each person can practice being interviewer, interviewee, and observer. You can work in groups of three for a total of 45 minutes (you might do this during a lunch hour), rotating through each interview and changing roles at approximate 15-minute intervals. You should plan for the interview itself to take 10 minutes.

Review the Interview Role Play script above before beginning the practice. Remember that the Interview Model can be applied to any number of topic areas: current job, previous jobs(s), education, career goals, leisure time, and the like.

The script is written so you can apply the Interview Model, acknowledge accomplishments, and probe limitations. You may also wish to probe accomplishments and try using stress and silence. Interviewers are urged to take notes throughout the interview.

Remember, this approach to interviewing is a *process*, and does not require a list of prepared questions and answers. Know what you want to learn about the candidate (imagine that you have a candidate/job profile), and select the topic areas that will cover the information you want. After your first Topic Opener Question(s), ask Self-Appraisal and Situation-Based Questions. They will help you gain a balanced picture of the person's Resume and Performance Factors (intellectual, interpersonal, motivational)—assessing both strengths and limitations.

If this were an actual interview, you would be filling out a balance sheet at the end. Be sure you take notes and gather enough information so you could do that.

When playing the role of Interviewee, help the interviewer learn and practice the Interview Model by answering as completely as possible, but also by being as natural as possible. Try handing back the Topic Opener Question: if the interviewer says, "Tell me about your current job" you can respond, "What would you like to know?" This will give the interviewer practice in handing the question back to you—and remind him/her not to qualify the Topic Opener Question and/or telegraph the answer. Give as much thought to your answers as if you were really interviewing for a job in your organization.

When playing the role of Observer, review the items on the following checklist before the start of the interview so you know what you are looking for. As observer, it is your job to provide constructive feedback to the interviewer you have just observed. When giving this feedback at the close of the interview, it is most helpful to start with the positive observations you made and to be as specific as possible. For example:

"I liked the way you led into the Self-Appraisal Question about his design award for his current work. You said, 'I was quite impressed by the award that you just described for your design work. What was it about your work that caused it to be recognized in this way?'"

"Your first Topic-Opener Question was excellent. You remembered that 'Tell me about your current job' is a good way to get a candidate to open up about what is important and provides you with excellent information to follow up on."

You can be direct in your suggestions about what could be done better, but be sure you have given positive feedback first:

"Your first Topic-Opener Question was very open, but your second one—'Tell me what your major was in college'—was too narrow. Had you said, 'Tell me about your college years', information about the major would have emerged. Remember the funnel or pie-piece model we used: the Topic Opener Question is at the top, and all other questions narrow and focus the information about the candidate."

"You had a terrific fact—his selection as youngest sales manager in the company—to explore with a Self-Appraisal Question. Think about how much more you might have learned about that fact if you had used one."

The following checklist will help observers know what to look for. It is also a good guide for checking yourself at the end of an actual interview—it will help you focus on the things you did well and the things you could have done better.

ROLE PLAY PRACTICE—OBSERVER'S CHECKLIST

1. The Interviewer used one or more Topic-Opener Questions. (Note topic or time period used.) ☐

2. The Interviewer used one or more Self-Appraisal Questions. (Note what fact the candidate was asked to explain.) ☐

3. The Interviewer probed accomplishments. (List accomplishments.) ☐

4. The Interviewer probed limitations. (Note which parts of the three-stage or other model the interviewer used.) ☐

5. The Interviewer used stress and/or silence appropriately. (Note where and how.) ☐

6. The Interviewer made the candidate comfortable and relaxed. (Note technique(s) used.) ☐

7. The Interviewer took notes throughout, and remembered to ask permission at the beginning of the interview. ☐

8. The Interviewee handed back at least one Broad-Brush Question. ☐

9. The Interviewer handed the Broad-Brush questions(s) back to the candidate (see 8, above). ☐

10. Things the Interviewer did particularly well were: (list)

11. Some things that need to be practiced were: (list)

Interviewer

_____

Observer

_____

Date _____

OTHER COMMENTS:

Appendix C

Sample Questions to Use in Conducting the Interview

The power of the Interview Model comes from the fact that it relies on a series of *question types* rather than a series of *questions and answers*. When you have become skilled in the use of the model, you will find that questions about the topics you select seem to form themselves from the candidate's answers. We do find, however, that people who are new to this way of interviewing appreciate having some examples to guide them.

The following questions can be drawn on when preparing for an interview. They include some of the sample questions that appear throughout the book, repeated here for your convenience.

The Interview Model—Sample Questions

Topic Opener

1. Tell me about your current job.

2. Tell me about your first job in this field.

3. Tell me about your career aspirations.

4. Tell me about your (college years) (graduate work).

5. Tell me about your leisure-time activities.

Self-Appraisal

Preface with statements like the following:

1. You mentioned that.....That's very impressive.

or

2. I see from your resume that....You must be very proud of that accomplishment.

Then ask one of the following:

1. What was it about you that enabled you to...?

or

2. Why do you suppose they (chose) (selected) (elected) you...?

or

3. How were you able to (achieve) (accomplish)....?

or

4. If I were to call up a former (boss) (professor) and ask what kind of (   ) you were, what do you suppose he/she would say?

or

5. What, would you say, is it about you that makes you successful at what you now do?

SITUATION-BASED

Problem Situation

1. What if you were in a situation where you had several important tasks to do and too little time to handle them all? How would you select which task(s) to do?

2. Have you ever had a situation where you had to resolve a conflict with a (client) (co-worker) (supervisor)? How did you resolve it?

3. Imagine a situation where you find yourself without the specific technical knowledge to perform a task essential to a project. What would you do?

4. Were you ever in a situation where you had to meet two different deadlines given to you by two different people and there wasn't time to do both? How did you handle the situation?

5. (Imagine you were) (Have you ever been) asked to (set up a project) (develop a sales territory) (introduce a new product) for which there was no organizational precedent to follow(.) (?) How (would) (did) you develop your plans?

Continuum

1. Where would you place yourself on a continuum from being a conceptual thinker to being an analytical thinker?

2. Where would you place yourself on a continuum from strategic planner at one end to pragmatic tactician at the other?

3. As you consider your most effective management style, place yourself on a continuum with managing ideas and concepts at one end and managing other people and their ideas at the other. Where would you place yourself?

4. How would you describe the energy you have as a point on a continuum: would it be marshalled intensively for specific projects or applied evenly across everything you do?

5. We all have our own way of getting things done—particularly when managing people. Someone once said that it all comes down to two basic styles: telling or selling. On a continuum, with *telling* at one end and *selling* at the other, how would you say you work with others to get results?

Comparison

1. Would you prefer to work for a boss whose strength is technical skills or one whose strength is managing and delegating?

2. If you had your choice, which would you prefer: a job with

a few big, solid long-term projects to concentrate on or one with many projects and shifting priorities?

3. Would you prefer to be in a situation where you were creating new markets or one where you were developing old ones?

4. When taking on a new project or task, do you generally like to have a great deal of feedback and supervision at the outset or do you like to figure it out for yourself and try your own approach?

5. When working with others on a project, do you generally prefer to communicate results and needs informally—phone calls or dropping by someone's office—or do you prefer to send memos?

Future Assessment

1. Let's imagine we've hired you, and you are having your (six-month) (one-year) performance review. What might (your boss) (I) say about your work during that review?

2. It's a year from now, and you've been with our organization long enough to know your job, and the culture. You're asked to do a self-assessment describing how you "fit in" here, and how well you're doing. What do you think you might say?

3. If I met you three years from now and you were disappointed in your progress in this organization, what might the reasons be?

For each of the question types for which examples have been given, you should develop several that fit your own style, personality and interviewing needs. The questions should be tailored to your organizational culture and reflect what you want to learn about each candidate.

The above questions, and the examples throughout the book, will help you apply the interview model while you are getting familiar with its use.

Questions That Explore Performance Factors

There are also questions that can help you resolve questions about the candidate's Performance Factors. These are drawn from materials prepared by PDP, Inc. of Woodland Park, Colorado and are used here with their permission. These questions are tied to the four behavorial trait areas defined in the section on the Interpersonal factor in Chapter 5, *The Performance Factors*.

Try using these questions when you know or suspect the named quality may be too *strong* for the job:

Dominance

1. How do you feel about taking directions from others and having them monitor your work?

2. In groups you were involved with in school, what role did you find yourself playing most frequently?

Extroversion

1. Have you ever been known to be overly enthusiastic in pursuing an activity? What were the others' responses?

2. Can you work productively without frequent exchange with or input from others?

Patience (Pace)

1. How do you feel about others pressuring you for deadlines? How have you reacted to such situations?

2. What is the ideal way to change a situation? How would you make this happen?

Conformity

1. How do you react to others when improvements are suggested for your work?

2. How does working without standard procedures appeal to you?

Use the following questions when you know or suspect the named quality may be too *low* for the job:

Dominance

1. What activities have you been in charge of organizing, setting up, and running?

2. How do you feel about giving directions to others and monitoring their work?

Extroversion

1. What is your view of dealing with people: trust and optimism, or realistically checking and being guarded in outlook?

2. How would you react to another's special request that was for personal reasons? How would you grant the request? How would you explain that to others who were not able to do the same thing? How would you handle denying the request?

Patience (Pace)

1. Describe a project or situation in which you thoroughly planned the start, steps, and outcome.

2. How do you feel about repeating an activity you have mastered once?

Conformity

1. How do you relate to being monitored in reviewing systems or procedures that you are supposed to follow?

2. Have you ever been in a situation where a project has been returned because of errors? What effect did this have on you?

PDP, Inc. has also developed questions for exploring a person's decision-making style. This helps you assess the Intellectual aspect of the Performance Factor. If you suspect a candidate uses more fact than feeling when making decisions or solving problems, try one of these questions:

1. What do you think of people who do not make decisions according to the facts?

2. What is the process by which you (make an important decision) (solve a problem).

If, on the other hand, you think the candidate relies more on feeling that fact, verify your concern by using one of these questions:

1. What is foremost in your mind when making decisions?

2. What has been your most successful decision? How did you make it? Why was it successful?

Finally, in assessing Motivation (another Performance Factor), energy plays a key role. If you are concerned the person has too much energy for the job, ask one of these questions:

1. What is your attitude towards someone who takes frequent breaks in a day and does not appear to be overly involved with the job?

2. Do you like to take on more than one project at a time? How do you manage them?

Or, if the person seems not to have enough energy, try to get a reading with one of the following questions:

1. Do you have any outside activities? How much time to you devote to these?

2. How do you relate to employees who take little time for breaks and take work home with them?

SUMMARY

The effectiveness of the behavorial interviewing model presented in this book depends on the use of *question types* rather than a series of *questions and answers*. However, these sample questions will help those learning to use the model, and should be considered a resource on which to draw. Similarly, using sample questions that help assess candidates with behavorial traits that seem too high or too low for the job can help you conduct more revealing interviews.

References

Blanchard, Kenneth, and Spencer Johnson. *The One Minute Manager*, ed. Pat Golbitz. New York: William Morrow, 1982.

Bloom, Benjamin. *Taxonomy of Educational Objectives, Handbook 1: Cognitive Domain*. White Plains, NY: Longman, 1977.

Deal, Terrence E., and Allan A. Kennedy. *Corporate Cultures: The Rites and Rituals of Corporate Life*. Reading, MA: Addison-Wesley, 1984.

Drucker, Peter. *Management: Tasks, Practices, Responsibilities*. New York: Harper & Row, 1974.

Fombrun, Charles, et al. *Strategic Human Resources Management*. New York: Wiley-Interscience, 1984.

Foulkes, Fred K. *Strategic Human Resource Management*. Englewood Cliffs, NJ: Prentice Hall, 1986.

Iacocca, Lee, and William Novack. *Iacocca: An Autobiography*. New York: Bantam, 1984.

Jackson, Tom. *Guerrilla Tactics in the Job Market*. New York: Bantam, 1978.

———. *The Perfect Resume*. New York: Doubleday, 1981.

Levering, Robert, et al. *One Hundred Best Companies to Work for in America*. Reading, MA: Addison-Wesley, 1984.

Lopez, Felix M., Jr. *Personnel Interviewing Theory and Practice*. New York: McGraw-Hill, 1975.

Medley, H. Anthony. *Sweaty Palms: The Neglected Art of Being Interviewed*. Belmont, CA: Lifetime Learning, 1978.

Merman, Stephen, and John McLaughlin. *Outinterviewing the Interviewer: The Job Winner's Script for Success*. Englewood Cliffs, NJ: Prentice Hall, 1982.

Peters, Thomas J., and Nancy K. Austin. *A Passion for Excellence: The Leadership Difference*. New York: Random House, 1985.

Peters, Tom, and Bob Waterman. *In Search of Excellence: Lessons From America's Best-Run Companies*. New York: Harper & Row, 1982.

Pettus, Theodore. *One on One: Win the Interview, Win the Job*. New York: Random House, 1981.

Wareham, John. *Secrets of a Corporate Headhunter*. New York: Atheneum, 1980.

Yeomans, William N. *One Thousand Things You Never Learned in Business School: How to Get Ahead of the Pack and Stay There*. New York: McGraw-Hill, 1984.

Index